THE CONFLICT WHISPERER

From Triggered to Transformed. A No-BS Guide to Managing Conflict in Every Relationship

By George L. Vergolias, Psy.D.
Executive & Life Coach
Clinical & Forensic Psychologist

Copyright, Legal Notice, and Disclaimer
Copyright © 2025 George L. Vergolias. All rights reserved.

No part of this workbook may be copied, reproduced, stored in a retrieval system, or transmitted in any form or by any means—electronic, mechanical, photocopying, recording, scanning, or otherwise—without prior written permission of the author or publisher, except as permitted by U.S. copyright law.

Legal Notice

This workbook is protected under copyright law. It is provided solely for personal use by the purchaser. You may not modify, distribute, sell, resell, share, quote extensively, or otherwise use the contents of this workbook without the express written consent of the author or publisher. Unauthorized use constitutes an infringement of copyright and may result in legal action.

Disclaimer Notice

The information contained in this workbook is provided for **educational and self-development purposes only**. It is **not medical, psychological, legal, or financial advice** and should not be relied upon as such. Use of this material does not create or imply any provider–patient, therapist–client, or other professional relationship between the reader and the author.

While every effort has been made to ensure accuracy and reliability, no representations or warranties of any kind are made, express or implied. The author and publisher disclaim any liability for any direct, indirect, incidental, or consequential damages, losses, or injuries resulting from the use or misuse of the information contained herein.

Readers are encouraged to seek the advice of qualified professionals (medical, mental health, legal, or financial, as appropriate) before making decisions or implementing strategies described in this workbook.

By using this workbook, you agree that the author and publisher shall not be held responsible for any errors, omissions, or outcomes related to the application of its content.

CONTENTS

INTRODUCTION --9
    Welcome from the Author -- 9
    Who This Workbook Is For -- 9
    How to Use This Workbook -- 10
    Why High-Achievers Struggle with Conflict -- 10
    The Cost of Avoided Conflict -- 11

01 Understanding Conflict -- 12
    1.1 What Is Conflict Really About? -- 12
    1.2 The Myths of Conflict -- 13
    1.3 Your Conflict Blueprint -- 14
    1.4 The 4 Default Conflict Responses -- 15
    1.5 Smart But Stuck: Why High-Achievers Struggle with Vulnerability -- 16
    1.6 The Escalation Cycle and The Rupture Curve: How Small Triggers Become Big Explosions -- 17
    1.7 Ego, Power & the Illusion of Control -- 20

02 Mastering Emotional Regulation -- 23
    2.1 The Science of Triggers and Emotional Hijacking -- 23
    2.2 Understanding Dysregulation: What Happens in the Brain & Body -- 25
    2.3 Breathing, Somatic Tools, and Nervous System Downshifting -- 27
    2.4 The Role of Shame, Guilt, and Anger in Conflict Cycles -- 33
    2.5 Mastering the Pause: Self-Regulation as a Power Move -- 35
    2.6 'I'm Not Mad!' – How Suppression Backfires: The Cost of 'Staying Cool' -- 37
    2.7 Teaching Regulation in Relationships: Modeling Calm -- 39

03 Communication Skills That Change Everything -- 41
    3.1 Why We Talk Past Each Other: Common Communication Blocks -- 41
    3.2 Active Listening as an Act of Leadership -- 43
    3.3 Speaking So You're Heard: Assertive vs. Aggressive vs. Passive -- 47
    3.4 The Power of Language: Framing and Reframing -- 51
    3.5. Repair Language: What to Say After a Blow-Up -- 52

04 The V.E.N.T. METHOD IN ACTION -- 55
    4.1 Overview of the V.E.N.T. Method™ -- 55
    4.2 V = Validate: The First De-escalation Tool -- 55
    4.3 E = Engage Curiously: Ask, Don't Accuse -- 56
    4.4 N = Navigate Needs: Unspoken Needs Fuel Ongoing Conflict -- 56
    4.5 T = Transform: Repair the Pattern, Don't Repeat It -- 57
    4.6 When V.E.N.T. Doesn't Work — Signs of Deeper Issues -- 58
    4.7 Practicing the Model with Real Scripts + Scenarios -- 58
    4.8 Real-Life Conflict Resolution Dialogues + Technique Breakdowns -- 59
    4.9 Core Needs Inventory –Worksheet -- 61

05 Boundaries That Actually Work 66
5.1 What Boundaries Really Are (and Aren't) 66
5.2 Why Most People Struggle to Set Boundaries 67
5.3 Internal vs. External Boundaries 69
5.4 The Consequences of Leaky and Rigid Boundaries 70

06 Conflict in Different Relationships 75
6.1 Conflict in Romantic Relationships: Attachment and Intimacy 75
6.2 Conflict During Separation & Divorce: The Rules Change 77
6.3 Friendship Conflicts: Betrayal, Ghosting, and Mismatched Expectations ... 79
6.4 Work Conflicts: Power, Politics, and Psychological Safety 80
6.5 Social Media, Digital Conflict, and 'Performative Outrage' 82
6.6 Gender, Identity & Emotional Labor in Conflict Dynamics 83

07 Mastering Conflict in High-Stakes Moments 85
7.1 What Makes a Moment 'High-Stakes' 85
7.2 Why Your Brain Hijacks You in Conflict 87
7.3 The Window of Tolerance (And Why You Leave It) 89
7.4 How to Recognize Fight, Flight, Freeze, Fawn 91

08 Repairing After Rupture 94
8.1 Why Repair Is More Important Than 'Never Fighting' 94
8.2 The Anatomy of a Rupture 96
8.3 Common Myths That Prevent Repair 97
8.4. How to Initiate Repair Without Losing Power 99

09 Preventing Conflict Before It Starts 101
9.1 The Hidden Triggers That Spark Conflict Early 101
9.2 What Psychological Safety Looks Like in Action 103
9.3 Proactive Communication Habits That Prevent Blowups 105
9.4 How to Build Trust Without Over-Explaining Yourself 109

10 Navigating Conflict During Separation and Divorce 111
10.1 Why Conflict During Divorce Feels So Personal (Even When It's Not) ... 111
10.2 The Push-Pull of Attachment and Autonomy in Separation 113
10.3 Common Communication Traps and How to Avoid Them 115
10.4 Navigating Co-Parenting with Boundaries, Not Bitterness 118

11 High-Conflict Personalities and How to Manage Them 121
11.1. What Is a High-Conflict Personality? (And What It's Not) 121
11.2 Why Logic and Empathy Often Backfire 124
11.3. The 4 Traits That Fuel High-Conflict Patterns: H.E.A.R.™ 125
11.4. How to Set Limits Without Escalating the Situation 127

12 Conflict with Yourself – From Inner Critic to Inner Peace 130
12.1 The War Within: Understanding Internal Conflict 130
12.2 Meet Your Inner Critic 132
12.3 From Self-Judgment to Self-Leadership 135

13 Repairing the Relationship With Yourself — 138
    13.1 The Rupture Within: Why We Turn Against Ourselves — 138
    13.2 The Power of Self-Forgiveness — 140
    13.3 Rebuilding Trust in Your Own Decision-Making — 142
    13.4 Cultivating Inner Safety and Integrity — 144

14 Creating a Conflict-Resilient Life — 147
    14.1 What Is a Conflict-Resilient Life? — 147
    14.2 Integrating Conflict Skills Into Everyday Life — 149
    14.3 Systems That Support Emotional Sustainability — 151

15 From Conflict to Growth — 154
    15.1 Boundaries: The Love Language of Self-Respect — 154
    15.2 Forgiveness Without Closure: Releasing What Hurts — 156
    15.3 Creating a Conflict Culture: With Family, Teams, Partners — 157
    15.4 Conflict as Intimacy, Growth, and Leadership — 160
    15.5 Building Your Personal Conflict Playbook — 162

16 The Conflict Whisperer's Toolkit — 166
    16.1 Quick-Reference Scripts: Communication on the Front Lines — 166
    16.2 Your Go-To Emergency De-escalation Strategies — 167
    16.3 Templates for Repair, Boundaries, and Clarifying Needs — 169

17 Your Conflict Mastery Plan — 172
    17.1 Reflecting on Your Journey — 172
    17.2 Your Personal Commitment Statement — 173
    17.3 Why Measuring Goals Matters for Real Change — 174
    17.4 Goal-Setting Prompts — 176
    17.5 Self-Assessment Checklist — 177

18 Final Reflections & Next Steps — 179
    Recap of the V.E.N.T. Method™ — 179
    Who You've Become Through This Work — 179
    Your Growth Isn't Just Yours: Spreading the Change — 180
    Invitation to Work Together: Coaching Support — 180

About the Author — 182
Addendum 1: Tools, Templates & Resources — 183
    Conflict Conversation Starters — 183
    30-Day Conflict Trigger Tracker — 184
    Boundary Setting Scripts — 185
    The Conflict Checklist — 185
    Reading List and Recommended Resources — 189

Addendum 2: Citations and Summary Notes — 190

LIST OF EXERCISES:

Exercise 1: Default Conflict Style Baseline (Section 1.3) --- 15
Exercise 2: Conflict Timeline Mapping (Section 1.4) --- 16
Exercise 3: Mapping Your Rupture Curve™ (Section 1.6) --- 18
Exercise 4: The Rupture Curve™ (Section 1.6) --- 19
Exercise 5: Journal Prompts: (Reflecting on Section 1) --- 21
Exercise 6: Mapping Your Trigger Landscape (Section 2.1) --- 24
Exercise 7: Nervous System Self-Assessment (Section 2.2) --- 26
Exercise 8: Somatic Reset Routine (Section 2.3) --- 32
Exercise 9: Emotional Triad Reflection (Section 2.4) --- 34
Exercise 10: The Power of the Pause (Section 2.5) --- 36
Exercise 11: Emotional Suppression Inventory (Section 2.6) --- 38
Exercise 12: Co-Regulation Check-In (Section 2.7) --- 40
Exercise 14: Identify Your Top 3 Communication Blocks (Section 3.1) --- 42
Exercise 15: Reflective Listening Practice (Section 3.2) --- 47
Exercise 16: Finding Your Assertive Voice (Section 3.3) --- 48
Exercise 17: Practicing Assertiveness (Chapter 3.3) --- 50
Exercise 18: Reframing Language (Section 3.4) --- 52
Exercise 19: Build Your Repair Toolkit (Section 3.5) --- 53
Exercise 20: V.E.N.T. Self-Reflection (Section 4) --- 63
Exercise 21: Reflective Journal Prompts (Section 4) --- 64
Exercise 22: Reframing Unhealthy Boundaries (Section 5.1) --- 67
Exercise 23: Confronting the Resistance to Set Boundaries (Section 5.2) --- 68
Exercise 24: Build Internal Boundaries First (Section 5.3) --- 70
Exercise 25: Recalibrate Your Boundary Style (Section 5.4) --- 71
Exercise 26: Reflective Journal Prompts (Section 5): --- 72
Exercise 27: Attachment Awareness Map (Section 6.1) --- 76
Exercise 28: Your Boundary Blueprint & Co-Parenting Comms Plan (Section 6.2) --- 78
Exercise 29: The Friendship Audit & Closure Letter (Section 6.3) --- 80
Exercise 30: Conflict Role-Play & Conflict Power Mapping (Section 6.4) --- 81
Exercise 31: Your Digital Delay Rule & Trigger Mapping (Section 6.5) --- 83
Exercise 32: Emotional Labor Log & Role Reversal Exercise (Section 6.6) --- 84
Exercise 33: Identify a High-Stakes Trigger (Section 7.1) --- 86
Exercise 34: Catching the Hijack (Section 7.2) --- 88

Exercise 35:	Practice Tool - Map Your Window of Tolerance (Section 7.3)	90
Exercise 36:	Know Your Stress Response Pattern (Section 7.4)	92
Exercise 37:	Personal Affirmation for Repair (Section 8.1)	95
Exercise 38:	Anatomy of a Rupture - Journal Prompt (Section 8.2)	97
Exercise 39:	Unpacking Your Repair Myths (Section 8.3)	98
Exercise 40:	Interpersonal Repair Script Practice (Section 8.4)	100
Exercise 41:	Create Your Trigger Map (Section 9.1)	102
Exercise 42:	Your Safety Contract (Section 9.2)	105
Exercise 43:	The Board Meeting (Section 9.3)	107
Exercise 44:	Your Escalation Prevention Ritual (Section 9.3)	108
Exercise 45:	One-Line Boundaries (Section 9.4)	110
Exercise 46:	The Conflict Letter (Section 10.1)	112
Exercise 47:	Mapping Attachment vs. Autonomy in Separation (Section 10.2)	114
Exercise 48:	Your Communication Reboot (Section 10.3)	117
Exercise 49:	The Co-Parenting Values Card (Section 10.4)	120
Exercise 50:	Conflict Pattern Tracker (Section 11.1)	122
Exercise 51:	The BIFF Method in action (Section 11.2)	125
Exercise 52:	H.E.A.R™ Cheat Sheet (Section 11.3)	126
Exercise 53:	Ready-To-Go Boundary Scripts (Section 11.4)	128
Exercise 54:	Align Your Internal Voice (Section 12.1)	131
Exercise 55:	Your Inner Critic Profile (Section 12.2)	134
Exercise 55:	Your Inner Critic Profile (Section 12.2)	135
Exercise 56:	Your Inner Critic Dialogue (Section 12.3)	136
Exercise 57:	Your Critic vs Advocate vs. Grounded Self Dialogue (Section 13.1)	139
Exercise 58:	Letter of Self-Forgiveness (Section 13.2)	142
Exercise 59:	Micro-Moments of Trust Log (Section 13.3)	143
Exercise 60:	The Integrity Inventory (Section 13.4)	145
Exercise 61:	Your Resilience Map (Section 14.1)	148
Exercise 62:	7-Day Habit Practice (Section 14.2)	150
Exercise 63:	Emotional Drains vs. Emotional Supports (Section 14.3)	152
Exercise 64:	Your Boundary Audit (Section 15.1)	155
Exercise 65:	The Letter of Release (Section 15.2)	157
Exercise 66:	Your Culture Map & Reset Ritual (Section 15.3)	158
Exercise 67:	Intimacy & Leadership Conflict Inventory (Section 15.4)	161
Exercise 68:	Your Conflict Playbook (Section 15.5)	164
Exercise 69:	Practice Quick-Reference Scripts (Section 16.1)	167
Exercise 70:	Your De-Escalation Plan (Section 16.2)	168

Exercise 71:   Your Go-To De-Escalation Templates (Section 16.3) -------------------- 170
Exercise 72:   Your Personal Commitment Statement (Section 17.2) ------------------ 174
Exercise 73:   Self-Assessment (Section 17.3) ---------------------------------- 175
Exercise 74:   Your 30-Day Growth Goal (Section 17.4) --------------------------- 177
Exercise 75:   Self-Assessment Checklist Review (Section 17.5) ------------------- 178

INTRODUCTION

WELCOME FROM THE AUTHOR

Let's be real—conflict sucks. And if you're anything like the high-achievers I coach, you've likely spent a good chunk of your life trying to outsmart, avoid, or power through it. I get it. I've been there. But here's what decades of clinical, forensic, and executive coaching work have taught me: **your relationships will only thrive to the degree that you're willing to face conflict head-on.**

This workbook isn't theory. It's field-tested. It's less focused on narrative, and more focused on practical exercises towards bringing massive change – because doing the work is what brings results. These tools have helped high-performing professionals, burned-out leaders, divorced parents, and quietly anxious perfectionists not just 'manage' conflict—but *transform* their relationship with it.

Whether you're flipping through this with curiosity or diving in out of desperation—welcome. You're in the right place.

WHO THIS WORKBOOK IS FOR

This workbook was designed for:

- High-achievers who want deeper, more authentic relationships but feel stuck in old patterns.

- Professionals who know how to lead in the boardroom but struggle to speak honestly at home.

- Men and women navigating the emotional wreckage of separation or divorce, who don't want to repeat the past.

- Anyone who wants to stop reacting impulsively and start responding with intention—even when triggered.

You don't have to be a psychologist, a coach, or a 'feelings person' to use this. You just need to be willing to get honest, do the work, and commit to something better than survival mode.

HOW TO USE THIS WORKBOOK

This is not a book you read once and shelf.

Each of the 14 sections is intentionally structured with:

- **Narrative lessons** rooted in clinical practice and coaching insight
- **Real-life case studies** to normalize and humanize growth
- **Research spotlights** so you understand the science behind your behavior
- **Coach's insights** to accelerate your progress
- **Exercises and journal prompts** to help you move from awareness to action

You can move through it sequentially or skip to the section where you're stuck (e.g., boundaries, divorce, inner critic). But don't just skim—*engage*. The breakthroughs happen when you apply what you learn to your real-life relationships.

Print it. Mark it up. Bring it into therapy. Discuss it with a coach. This is your playbook for transformation.

WHY HIGH-ACHIEVERS STRUGGLE WITH CONFLICT

High-performers are rewarded for control, composure, and getting results. But conflict—especially relational conflict—is messy, emotional, and nonlinear. It threatens the very identity you've worked so hard to build.

Many high-achievers struggle because:

- They've been taught that emotion = weakness.
- They equate vulnerability with loss of power.
- They're great at solving problems—but not at tolerating emotional ambiguity.
- Their nervous system is wired for performance, not intimacy.

What got you success in your career might be sabotaging your connection at home.

This workbook will help you rewrite that wiring—without losing your edge.

THE COST OF AVOIDED CONFLICT

Here's the truth: *What you don't address will eventually erode your peace, your productivity, and your relationships.*

- 70% of workplace conflict is due to miscommunication or unspoken needs (CPP Global Human Capital Report, 2020).

- In romantic relationships, unaddressed conflict is the #1 predictor of emotional disengagement and divorce (Gottman Institute, 2019).

- Chronic conflict avoidance is linked to higher rates of anxiety, suppressed anger, and even cardiovascular issues (APA, 2015).

- Teams that avoid hard conversations underperform by up to 35% compared to conflict-resilient teams (Harvard Business Review, 2022).

Avoidance feels easier in the short term. But it comes at a long-term cost to your health, your leadership, and your emotional integrity.

You didn't come here for fluff. You came to level up.

Let's begin!

George J. V. Vergolias, PsyD
CEO | Executive & Life Coach

SECTION 1:
UNDERSTANDING CONFLICT

'Your success is almost exclusively tied to the degree to which you can keep a promise to yourself.'
~ Gary John Bishop

'What makes great relationships great is not that you get along all the time. The best marriages, the best relationships, they aren't free of conflict – it's that they know how to resolve conflict peacefully.'
~ Simon Sinek

1.1 WHAT IS CONFLICT REALLY ABOUT?

Conflict is often mistaken for dysfunction. Many believe that a relationship filled with arguments, disagreements, or emotional tension is broken. But conflict isn't the enemy — disconnection is.

At its core, conflict arises from two psychological events: the perception of threat and the breakdown of emotional connection. The moment we believe something important — our safety, identity, values, or sense of worth — is being challenged, we feel emotionally triggered. When that activation is combined with an inability to communicate or be understood, conflict escalates.

In high-functioning individuals, this conflict is often masked under control, avoidance, or intellectualization. Rather than shouting, they shut down or withdraw emotionally. Rather than seeking resolution, they seek superiority or distance.

COACH'S INSIGHT

Most arguments aren't about what they seem to be about. It's rarely about the dishes, the email tone, or the missed deadline. It's about feeling unseen, unheard, or unimportant. Once you understand this, your entire view of conflict shifts.

RESEARCH SPOTLIGHT

According to Dr. John Gottman's research, nearly 69% of recurring issues in relationships are 'perpetual problems' — issues rooted in personality or value differences that never fully go away. The difference between healthy and toxic conflict is not whether the issue is solved, but whether emotional safety is maintained during the process (Gottman, 1999).

CASE STUDY

Samantha, a 39-year-old executive, came to coaching after repeated breakdowns in her romantic relationship. Her partner complained that she was emotionally unavailable. In sessions, it became clear that Samantha feared vulnerability. She treated conflict like a corporate negotiation: dissecting problems without ever expressing personal emotion. Through targeted work on emotional literacy, Samantha learned to name what she felt — which allowed connection to replace criticism.

1.2 THE MYTHS OF CONFLICT

Myth #1: *Conflict Means the Relationship Is Broken*

> Reality: Conflict is normal. In fact, its absence can indicate avoidance, emotional suppression, or disengagement. Couples and teams that communicate openly — even when it's uncomfortable — demonstrate higher levels of trust and intimacy.

Myth #2: *Avoiding Conflict Preserves Harmony*

> Reality: Avoidance is often self-protective in the short term, but ultimately destructive. Over time, it breeds resentment, miscommunication, and emotional detachment. What goes unspoken festers.

Myth #3: *High Performers Don't Struggle with Conflict*

> Reality: High performers are often rewarded for control and problem-solving, not vulnerability. They may intellectualize, suppress, or power through emotional tension — making them ill-equipped to manage relational conflict in emotionally honest ways.

RESEARCH SPOTLIGHT

A *Harvard Business Review* study (2017) found that teams with higher psychological safety — where conflict was addressed openly — performed significantly better and had lower turnover. Avoidance, on the other hand, correlated with lower innovation and trust.

CASE STUDY

David, a 47-year-old founder of a tech startup, struggled with staff turnover and dissatisfaction. In coaching, it became evident that he avoided confrontation, assuming it would hurt morale. In reality, his lack of feedback left employees anxious and unclear about expectations. Once he began delivering clear, compassionate feedback, engagement improved dramatically.

1.3 YOUR CONFLICT BLUEPRINT

Every person carries an unconscious script about how to handle conflict — a script shaped by our earliest experiences. This 'conflict blueprint' is influenced by family dynamics, cultural beliefs, early traumas, and modeled behaviors.

For example, if you grew up in a household where emotions were punished, you may have learned that silence equals safety. If one parent yelled and the other withdrew, you may associate conflict with volatility or abandonment.

Common Blueprint Influences:

- Family communication patterns
- Cultural norms around emotion and authority
- Childhood attachment style
- Early trauma or neglect
- Gender role expectations

COACH'S INSIGHT

We don't just inherit eye color or personality from our parents — we inherit how they handled tension, disagreement, and repair. Your adult relationship patterns are often echoes of those early blueprints.

RESEARCH SPOTLIGHT

Attachment theory research shows that early caregiver interactions influence how we manage closeness and conflict. Insecurely attached individuals (anxious or avoidant) often struggle with either fear of abandonment or discomfort with emotional closeness, both of which shape conflict behaviors (Mikulincer & Shaver, 2007).

CASE STUDY

Lena, a 33-year-old attorney, avoided raising concerns with her partner. She feared she'd seem 'needy' or 'too much.' In her family, emotions were minimized, and her needs were often unmet. Coaching helped Lena identify this pattern and learn to express her needs without guilt or self-editing.

Exercise 1: Default Conflict Style Baseline (Section 1.3)

Measure common conflict responses to get an initial baseline of your default conflict style.

Instructions: Check off what you do most often in conflict situations.

Behavior	Never	Sometimes	Often	Always
Raise my voice	☐	☐	☐	☐
Shut down emotionally	☐	☐	☐	☐
Use sarcasm or passive-aggression	☐	☐	☐	☐
Avoid the person entirely	☐	☐	☐	☐
Apologize to keep the peace	☐	☐	☐	☐
Blame others quickly	☐	☐	☐	☐

1.4 THE 4 DEFAULT CONFLICT RESPONSES

When conflict arises, your nervous system responds automatically. These reactions — known as fight, flight, freeze, or fawn — are rooted in your autonomic nervous system, which is designed to protect you from perceived threat.

Fight: Aggression, dominance, criticism
Flight: Avoidance, distraction, leaving the room
Freeze: Emotional shutdown, numbness, indecision
Fawn: Over-accommodation, people-pleasing, self-abandonment

These are adaptive survival responses — not personality flaws. But when left unexamined, they limit intimacy and resolution.

Quick Self-Check:

- Which response do you default to in conflict?
- Do you shift responses in different relationships?
- What does each response protect you from feeling?

RESEARCH SPOTLIGHT

Dr. Stephen Porges' Polyvagal Theory explains how our body's nervous system evaluates risk and chooses a response — often below the level of consciousness. Our ability to regulate and shift out of these responses is key to repairing conflict and restoring connection.

CASE STUDY

Jordan, a high-performing sales executive, experienced emotional 'freeze' in conflict with his partner. He'd go silent, not out of indifference, but because he felt overwhelmed and dissociated. Through coaching, he learned grounding techniques and ways to signal safety through nonverbal connection.

Exercise 2 : Conflict Timeline Mapping (Section 1.4)

Instructions: Draw a timeline of 5–7 major conflicts you've experienced (at home, work, or in friendships).

For each conflict, note:

- What triggered the conflict? _____
- How did you respond? _____
- What emotions or needs were beneath your response? _____
- How was it resolved (or not)? _____
- What would you do differently now? _____

1.5 SMART BUT STUCK: WHY HIGH-ACHIEVERS STRUGGLE WITH VULNERABILITY

High achievers are often rewarded for controlling outcomes, thinking rationally, and driving performance. But those strengths can become liabilities in emotionally charged situations. When conflict arises, the tendency to 'fix' rather than 'feel' can shut down meaningful dialogue.

Vulnerability isn't inefficiency — it's relational currency. Without it, conflict resolution remains transactional. High performers may default to defensiveness, blame, or problem-solving instead of emotional transparency. But emotional exposure is what transforms conflict into connection.

COACH'S INSIGHT

Being in control and being connected aren't always the same thing. High-performers often confuse emotional control with strength — but the real flex is learning how to express needs without shame.

CASE STUDY

Raj, a 45-year-old executive, avoided discussing emotional tension with his wife, believing it would derail his focus. In coaching, he discovered that his drive to perform came from childhood pressure to be the 'strong one.' Naming that origin story allowed him to practice vulnerability — not just with his wife, but with himself.

1.6 THE ESCALATION CYCLE AND THE RUPTURE CURVE: HOW SMALL TRIGGERS BECOME BIG EXPLOSIONS

Most major blow-ups don't start big — they start with a micro-trigger: a sigh, a tone, a glance. We tell ourselves a story, react to that story, and the tension snowballs. This process is what I call the Rupture Curve™.

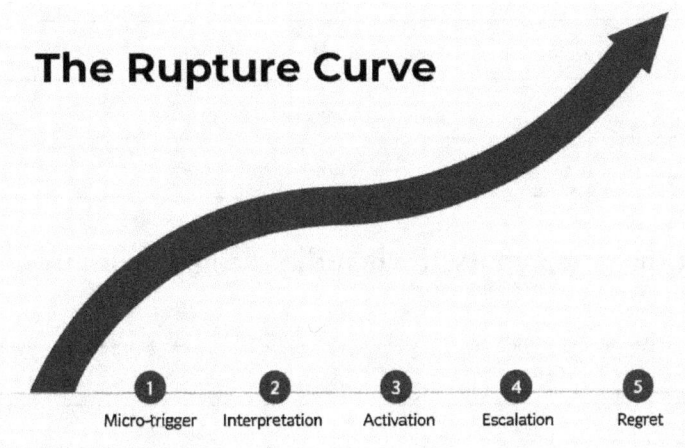

1. **Micro-trigger** — Something small touches a nerve.
2. **Interpretation** — You assign meaning: disrespect, abandonment, control.
3. **Activation** — Emotional arousal spikes; nervous system floods.
4. **Reaction** — Fight, flight, freeze, or fawn kicks in.
5. **Escalation** — Misunderstanding compounds; emotions spiral.
6. **Regret** — Disconnection deepens unless repair is initiated.

RESEARCH SPOTLIGHT

Neuroscientist Dr. Dan Siegel describes this as 'flipping your lid' — when the brain's pre-frontal cortex (rational thought) gets hijacked by the amygdala (emotional reactivity). This explains why conflict often feels irrational in the moment.

CASE STUDY

Tina and Leo had a recurring argument about dinner plans. On the surface, it seemed petty, but the deeper trigger for Tina was feeling deprioritized. For Leo, it was about autonomy. Once they learned to spot the trigger-interrupt-react cycle, their arguments became shorter — and sometimes even productive.

Exercise 3: Mapping Your Rupture Curve™ (Section 1.6)

Using a blank sheet or the space below, recreate your personal escalation (rupture) curve by answering:

1. What small behaviors or micro-triggers tend to set you off?

_____

_____

_____

_____

2. What story do you usually tell yourself when those triggers occur?

_____

_____

_____

_____

3. How do you feel physically and emotionally during activation?

_____

_____

_____

_____

4. What does your reaction look like?

_____

_____

_____

_____

5. What are the consequences or regrets that follow?

_____

_____

_____

_____

6. Where can you intervene earlier next time?

_____

_____

_____

_____

Exercise 4: The Rupture Curve™ (Section 1.6)

Reference the graphic, with a curve rising sharply from left to right, representing:

1. Micro-trigger
2. Interpretation
3. Activation
4. Reaction
5. Escalation
6. Regret

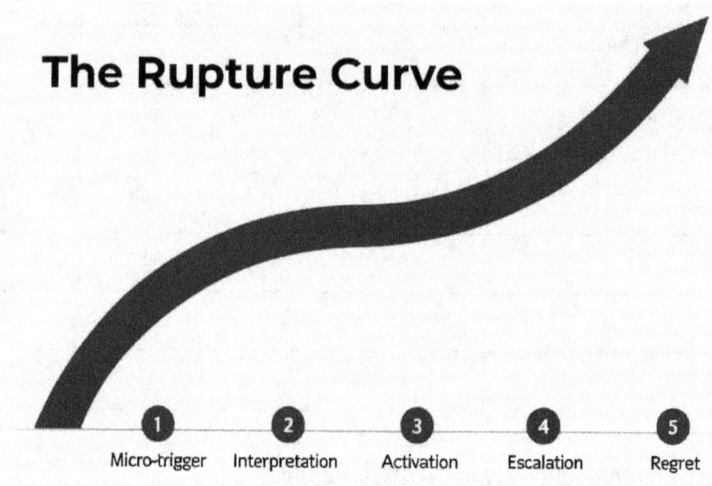

Use this curve to map your personal escalation cycle and identify where to pause, reframe, or self-regulate.

1.7 EGO, POWER & THE ILLUSION OF CONTROL

In conflict, your ego wants three things: to be right, to win, and to avoid blame. But conflict isn't a courtroom. It's a crucible for connection.

Power struggles are often masked bids for control — over outcomes, emotions, or how the other person sees us. True resolution comes when you release the illusion of control and instead aim for influence and empathy.

Control says: 'I need to fix you to feel safe.'

Empathy says: 'I can tolerate your difference and still stay connected.'

COACH'S INSIGHT

Your ego will tell you that winning the argument is worth it. But winning at the cost of the relationship is just losing in disguise.

CASE STUDY

Angela, a COO, kept trying to 'correct' her partner's feedback style. In reality, she was trying to protect her ego from vulnerability. When she shifted from correction to curiosity, her relationship dynamics transformed.

Exercise 5: Journal Prompts: (Reflecting on Section 1)

What was your family's pattern around conflict when you were growing up?

_____
_____
_____
_____

Which of the four default conflict responses (fight, flight, freeze, fawn) do you use most and in what context?

_____
_____
_____
_____

When was the last time you felt emotionally hijacked during a conflict? What triggered it, and how did you respond?

_____
_____
_____
_____

What beliefs about conflict were passed down to you — and which of those do you want to release or rewrite?

_____
_____
_____
_____

What would it look like to respond to conflict with curiosity instead of control?

_____

_____

_____

_____

What does your ego protect you from feeling — and how does that affect your approach to disagreement?

_____

_____

_____

_____

SECTION 2:
MASTERING EMOTIONAL REGULATION

'You can't solve a conflict from a nervous system that's in survival mode.'
~ **Dr. George Vergolias**

2.1 THE SCIENCE OF TRIGGERS AND EMOTIONAL HIJACKING

A trigger is any stimulus—external or internal—that activates a rapid, intense emotional reaction. Triggers are often rooted in previous experiences, unresolved trauma, attachment wounds, or deeply held beliefs. While triggers vary by individual, the response they provoke is usually universal: an immediate shift into defense or survival mode.

When we are triggered, the brain's limbic system takes over. The amygdala, a structure responsible for detecting threats, hijacks the prefrontal cortex—our center for logic, reasoning, and executive function. This results in what Daniel Goleman coined an 'amygdala hijack,' where emotion overrides cognition.

Emotional hijacking occurs when the brain's amygdala overrides the rational prefrontal cortex. In conflict, this looks like yelling, shutting down, defensiveness, or panic — not because we want to act that way, but because our body perceives danger, not dialogue.

None of us are immune to this hijacking, even if you are a high performer or very successful person. High performers may be excellent under pressure at work, but when the conflict touches something personal — fear of rejection, criticism, or powerlessness — the hijack can be swift and invisible.

This is why you may say things you don't mean or shut down and dissociate mid-argument. It's not about willpower. It's biology.

RESEARCH SPOTLIGHT

The amygdala processes threat signals in 12 milliseconds—much faster than the cortex, which takes about 300 milliseconds to form a rational response (LeDoux, 1996). This makes early emotional reactions feel uncontrollable because they often are.

Daniel Goleman coined the term 'amygdala hijack' to describe this state of emotional flooding where the brain reacts before rational thought can intervene. It's not weakness — it's biology.

COACH'S INSIGHT

The moment you feel hijacked, ask: *'What part of me is trying to protect me right now?'* This creates distance from the trigger and shifts you back into self-awareness.

CASE STUDY

After being interrupted in meetings, Emma—a senior project manager—would lash out sharply. In coaching, she connected this to childhood memories of not being allowed to speak. With practice, she learned to pause and name her emotion before reacting. This built emotional safety with her team and helped her feel more in control of her own reactions.

Mark, a 40-year-old finance director, would become disproportionately angry when his team challenged his ideas. In coaching, we traced this reaction back to childhood experiences of being dismissed by a critical father. Once he recognized the emotional link, he could pause and regulate — instead of reacting with aggression.

Exercise 6: Mapping Your Trigger Landscape (Section 2.1)

Instructions: Reflect on the moments in your personal or professional life where you felt emotionally hijacked. Identify the trigger, the initial reaction, and the outcome.

Then consider what need or wound might have been activated.

- What are your top 3 emotional triggers?

1. _____
2. _____
3. _____

- What types of people, tones, or behaviors tend to activate you?

1. _____
2. _____
3. _____

What are the deeper themes beneath these triggers (e.g., rejection, disrespect, abandonment)?

_____
_____
_____
_____

2.2 UNDERSTANDING DYSREGULATION: WHAT HAPPENS IN THE BRAIN & BODY

Emotional dysregulation refers to a state in which our physiological arousal interferes with our ability to think, listen, or respond effectively. When dysregulated, the sympathetic nervous system takes over, releasing stress hormones like adrenaline and cortisol.

This emotional dysregulation is the body's stress response; it is an attempt to regulate and control the situation. One way to think about it, it is a normative evolutionary response to an abnormal (non-common) situation. Heart rate rises, breathing becomes shallow, and the nervous system prepares for fight, flight, freeze, or fawn. This is not a choice — it's an involuntary survival system.

This is when your palms sweat, your heart races, and your ability to speak clearly disappears. Your system isn't broken—it's doing its job. The key is learning how to recognize and intervene before reactivity takes the wheel.

In conflict, dysregulation narrows our perspective. We stop listening. We interpret tone as threat. We misread intent. Regulation isn't about calming down — it's about regaining access to the part of your brain that can connect, empathize, and reason.

Dysregulation also makes it harder to hear others accurately. Our brain scans for threats, not nuance. Tone, facial expressions, and intentions get misread. Over time, this leads to chronic miscommunication and emotional burnout in relationships.

RESEARCH SPOTLIGHT

Polyvagal Theory (Porges, 2011) describes how the vagus nerve influences our ability to feel safe. A regulated nervous system supports connection, while a dysregulated one prepares us for defense—even when no real threat exists.

COACH'S INSIGHT

The more you can recognize dysregulation in real time, the less likely you are to damage trust or escalate tension. Self-awareness is the precursor to self-regulation.

You can't regulate your partner's emotions — but you can regulate your own. And doing so often shifts the entire dynamic.

CASE STUDY

Miguel, a corporate team leader, found that after client meetings he would often feel exhausted and irritable. Tracking his state with a regulation journal revealed that he was spending hours in low-level fight-or-flight mode. Through body scans and micro-breaks, he learned to downshift his system—improving both mood and clarity.

RESEARCH SPOTLIGHT

The autonomic nervous system governs our stress response. Polyvagal Theory (Porges, 2011) emphasizes how 'neuroception'— the brain's unconscious detection of safety or danger — drives our physiological state in conflict.

Exercise 7: Nervous System Self-Assessment (Section 2.2)

Instructions: Over the next week, track your nervous system states. Use the table below to log moments when you felt dysregulated, and what helped you return to calm. Use checkmarks or color coding.

Sample Tracking Table:

Time	Trigger	Physical Sensation	Emotional State	Regulation Tool Used	Outcome

2.3 BREATHING, SOMATIC TOOLS, AND NERVOUS SYSTEM DOWNSHIFTING

You can't think your way out of an emotional flood — you have to feel your way through it. Somatic tools help us shift our nervous system from activation (fight/flight/freeze) to regulation (calm/present/connected).

The nervous system speaks through sensation. When your stomach tightens or your shoulders clench, your body is sending a signal: 'I'm not safe.' You don't need to argue with the signal — you need to respond to it and manage it.

These somatic practices work directly with the body to reduce arousal and restore inner safety. Over time, using these tools creates a feedback loop — your body learns that it can return to safety, even in conflict.

COACH'S INSIGHT

If you wait until you're overwhelmed to regulate, you've waited too long. Build in somatic practices *before* the storm.

RESEARCH SPOTLIGHT

A 2018 study published in *Frontiers in Human Neuroscience*, Zaccaro and colleagues found that deep breathing reduced sympathetic nervous system activity and increased vagal tone — a key indicator of resilience and emotional flexibility.

CASE STUDY

Jessica, a trial lawyer, felt trapped in emotional shutdown during arguments with her spouse. With coaching, she began a 5-minute morning practice of grounding and breathwork. She reported greater self-awareness and a dramatic decrease in reactive outbursts — not just at home, but in court.

Talia, a 29-year-old attorney, struggled with panic during conflict. She learned to excuse herself briefly to do deep breathing before returning to a conversation. Her ability to self-regulate transformed her confidence in difficult discussions.

Practical Somatic Tools for Self-Regulation

The fastest way to regulate emotion is through the body — not the brain. Breathing techniques, movement, grounding exercises, and somatic awareness can interrupt the stress cycle and restore a sense of internal safety.

The following are easy to implement breathing and somatic techniques that help with emotional regulation:

- **Box Breathing:** For a count of 4 seconds at each stage: Inhale (4s) – Hold (4s) – Exhale (4s) – Hold (4s). Repeat this cycle 4 times. It intentionally and steadily slows down and regulates your breathing. As your physical regulation goes, so will your mental and emotional regulation follow.

- **5-4-3-2-1 Grounding:** Name 5 things you **see**; 4 you can **touch**; 3 you **hear**; 2 you **smell**; 1 you **taste**. By focusing on our senses, it gets us out of our heads and away from anxiety-provoking thoughts.

- **Physiological Sigh:**

  The **physiological sigh** is a natural breathing pattern—a long full inhale, followed immediately by a short, quick additional inhale to maximum lung capacity, then followed by a long, slow exhale—that the body uses spontaneously to reduce stress and restore balance to the nervous system. It stimulates the **vagus nerve** and activates the parasympathetic branch, helping lower heart rate, reduce anxiety, and regulate emotional states. This technique has been shown in research to rapidly decrease physiological arousal and improve calm focus in under a minute.

  ### Benefits include:

  - **Rapid stress reduction** — calms the body after a stress spike.
  - **Improved vagal tone** — supports emotional regulation and resilience.
  - **Lowered heart rate and blood pressure** — especially helpful in moments of tension.
  - **Enhanced focus** — resets mental clarity in high-pressure situations.

How to Do the Physiological Sigh

1. **First Inhale:** Take a deep breath through your nose, filling your lungs about 90%.
2. **Second Inhale:** Without exhaling, take a short, quick *top-up* inhale also through your nose to fully inflate your lungs.
3. **Long Exhale:** Slowly and fully exhale through your mouth (preferably with pursed lips) until your lungs feel empty.
4. **Repeat:** Perform **1–3 cycles** as needed to feel calmer.

Pro Tip: Focus on the *long, controlled exhale*—this is what maximizes vagus nerve activation and the calming effect.

- **Shaking:** Loosen limbs to release excess activation (used in trauma recovery models).

Shaking is a simple somatic technique inspired by natural stress-release behaviors in animals. After a threat passes, many animals instinctively shake or tremble to discharge excess adrenaline and reset the nervous system. For humans, deliberate shaking can help release muscular tension, reduce the physiological effects of stress, and stimulate vagus nerve activity by shifting the body from a fight-or-flight state into parasympathetic recovery.

Benefits include:

- **Nervous system reset** — helps 'complete' the stress response and return to calm.
- **Reduced muscle tension** — loosens areas where stress is stored.
- **Improved mood** — promotes endorphin release and a sense of lightness.
- **Enhanced vagal tone** — supports emotional regulation and resilience.

How to Do Shaking for Vagus Nerve Activation

1. Find a safe space where you can move freely without obstacles.
2. Stand with feet shoulder-width apart, knees slightly bent, and arms relaxed.
3. Start gently bouncing through the knees, letting your body move loosely.
4. Let the movement travel upward — allow your shoulders, arms, chest, and head to shake naturally.
5. Release control — imagine stress, tension, or heaviness leaving your body with each movement.
6. Continue for 1–3 minutes (or longer if comfortable), keeping your breath easy and natural.
7. Finish by slowing down gradually, then pause for a few breaths, noticing the sensations of calm and relaxation.

Pro Tip: You can combine shaking with music to make it more engaging or use it as a quick reset between stressful meetings or events.

Humming:

Humming is a simple yet powerful way to stimulate the vagus nerve through vibration of the vocal cords and resonance in the chest, throat, and face. Because the vagus nerve passes near the larynx and pharynx, humming directly engages it, sending calming signals to the brain and body. Research shows that vocal toning, chanting, and humming can increase heart rate variability (HRV), lower stress, and improve emotional regulation.

Benefits include:

- **Parasympathetic activation** — promotes relaxation and calm.
- **Stress reduction** — lowers heart rate and blood pressure.
- **Improved mood** — vibrations release nitric oxide, which enhances circulation and supports a sense of well-being.
- **Accessible anywhere** — no equipment needed, can be used discreetly.

How to Do Humming for Vagus Nerve Activation

1. **Find a comfortable position** — sitting or standing upright with relaxed shoulders.
2. **Inhale deeply** through your nose.
3. **Exhale slowly while humming** (like the sound "mmm") until all the air is released.
4. **Feel the vibration** in your chest, throat, and face — focus on the resonance.
5. **Repeat for 1–5 minutes**, staying relaxed and breathing naturally between hums.
6. **Optional variation:** Close your eyes and place a hand on your chest to deepen the calming effect.

Pro Tip: A low, steady tone works best. You can also hum along with calming music or try extended humming (longer exhale than inhale) to amplify vagus nerve stimulation.

- **Cold Exposure:** Cold exposure can help regulate vagus nerve activation by stimulating the parasympathetic nervous system, which promotes relaxation, improved emotional regulation, and reduced stress responses. When the body is exposed to cold—such as through cold showers, ice baths, or even splashing cold water on the face—it triggers the **diving reflex,** a physiological response that slows the heart rate, constricts blood vessels, and enhances vagal tone.

Why does cold exposure work?

Cold exposure stimulates skin thermoreceptors, triggering the diving reflex and increasing vagal tone. Over time, this can improve stress regulation, mood stability, heart rate variability, and recovery capacity.

Benefits include:

- **Improved stress resilience:** Enhances the body's ability to return to a calm baseline after stress.

- **Better emotional regulation:** Supports a balanced autonomic nervous system, reducing anxiety and emotional reactivity.

- **Enhanced recovery:** Promotes anti-inflammatory effects and may improve immune function.

- **Greater heart rate variability (HRV):** A sign of stronger vagal tone and cardiovascular health.

Cold Exposure Protocol for Vagus Nerve Activation

1. Start Small & Controlled

    - Begin with cold face immersion or cold-water splash:

    - Fill a sink or bowl with cool water (50–60°F / 10–15°C).

    - Submerge your face for 10–15 seconds, or splash cold water over the cheeks, forehead, and neck 5–10 times.

    - This activates the *mammalian diving reflex*, stimulating the vagus nerve.

2. Transition to Cold Showers

    - End your normal warm shower with 20–30 seconds of cold water (start lukewarm if needed).

    - Over time, work up to 1–2 minutes at a tolerable cold temperature.

    - Breathe slowly and deeply—don't hold your breath, as calm breathing strengthens the parasympathetic response.

3. Optional: Ice Bath / Cold Plunge (Advanced)

- For those healthy and acclimated, 1–3 minutes in water between 50–59°F (10–15°C) is sufficient.
- Focus on *calm exhalations* and keeping shoulders relaxed.

4. Frequency

- 2–4 times per week for most benefit; daily brief exposure is fine if well-tolerated.

5. Safety Guidelines

- It is recommended always to consult your physician before taking on any change in health regimen, including cold exposure
- Avoid if you have uncontrolled cardiovascular conditions, Raynaud's disease, or cold urticaria.
- Always exit if you feel dizzy, numb, or short of breath beyond the initial shock.
- Never combine with breath-holding in water (risk of shallow-water blackout).

Exercise 8: Somatic Reset Routine (Section 2.3)

Instructions: Select two somatic tools and integrate them into your daily routine. Practice at neutral times and during minor conflict.

Examples include box breathing, cold water on face, humming, or shaking.

- Tool 1: _____ | Daily Time: _____
- Tool 2: _____ | Daily Time: _____
- Observed effects after 3 days: _____

2.4 THE ROLE OF SHAME, GUILT, AND ANGER IN CONFLICT CYCLES

Conflict often uncovers more than disagreement — it unearths emotional landmines like shame, guilt, and anger.

- Guilt is the belief that you **DID** something wrong or bad.
- Shame is the belief that you **ARE** unworthy or bad.
- Anger often masks both —and serves as a protector.

Shame says: *'I am bad'*.

Guilt says: *'I did something bad'*.

Anger says: *'Someone wronged me'*.

All three emotions show up in conflict, often masked as defensiveness, withdrawal, or aggression.

Many high-functioning individuals are masters of hiding shame. They overperform, over-control, or overplease in an effort to never feel like a disappointment. When conflict arises, their response is often extreme: defensiveness, blame-shifting, or retreat.

Many high achievers struggle with internalized shame — a belief that they must earn love, respect, or safety. When conflict threatens their self-image, shame hijacks their ability to stay present. Others bury guilt beneath blame. Some weaponize anger as protection.

Understanding the roots of these emotions helps us respond to what's underneath the behavior — in ourselves and others.

Learning to decode these emotional drivers helps us communicate authentically — and repair instead of repeat.

COACH'S INSIGHT

Shame thrives in secrecy. Bringing it into the light — even privately — starts the process of transformation.

RESEARCH SPOTLIGHT

According to Dr. Brené Brown's research (2012), people who are able to identify and express guilt (vs. shame) are more likely to take responsibility, repair relationships, and exhibit empathy. Guilt, when processed healthily, is a social glue. Shame isolates.

CASE STUDY

Andre, a physician and father of three, constantly felt 'not good enough' in both roles. He reacted to any criticism from his wife with withdrawal or rage. Coaching revealed deep shame rooted in childhood rejection. Naming that pattern gave him space to feel guilt without collapsing into shame — and allowed him to engage in conflict without fear of being 'found out' as flawed.

Exercise 9: Emotional Triad Reflection (Section 2.4)

Instructions: Choose a recent conflict and break it down using the Shame-Guilt-Anger triad. This helps separate feeling from identity and enables emotional processing.

Then reflect:

What emotion showed up first?

_____

_____

What emotion was hidden underneath?

What message or belief was attached to that emotion?

2.5 MASTERING THE PAUSE: SELF-REGULATION AS A POWER MOVE

In conflict, milliseconds matter. The pause is your moment of power — the brief space between being triggered and choosing your next move.

When you pause, you interrupt the automatic pattern of defense and give your rational mind time to catch up. This creates the possibility for a different outcome.

The pause is not silence. It's presence. It's breath. It's grounding. It's awareness. Learning to pause doesn't mean you suppress your reaction. It means you're creating a container to hold your reaction until you can respond from clarity rather than chaos.

RESEARCH SPOTLIGHT

Neuroscientific research by Dr. Richard Davidson (2012) at the University of Wisconsin-Madison shows that individuals who regularly practice mindfulness — which strengthens the pause — display greater activation in the prefrontal cortex and reduced amygdala activity over time.

COACH'S INSIGHT

The Power of the Pause: The moment you pause, you change the entire trajectory of the interaction. That's power. Not control over others — but mastery of self.

CASE STUDY

Lauren, a director of operations, had a habit of interrupting when she felt misunderstood. By practicing a 3-second pause and grounding breath before responding, she noticed that 70% of her emotional reactivity disappeared. Her team became more open and less defensive, and Lauren's credibility grew.

Exercise 10: The Power of the Pause (Section 2.5)

Instructions: Practice inserting a 3–5 second pause in low-stakes conversations. The reason to start with low-stakes conflict is that these are far less likely to escalate and trigger you quickly. As you grow more proficient with the pause, you can apply it to a broader range of conversations and conflict situations.

Track your experience over time:

- How did it feel to pause?

_____
_____
_____
_____

- What did you notice about the other person's response?

_____
_____
_____
_____

- Did your outcome improve?

_____
_____

2.6 'I'M NOT MAD!' – HOW SUPPRESSION BACKFIRES: THE COST OF 'STAYING COOL'

'I'm fine.'

How often do you say this when you're not?

Emotional suppression — especially common among high achievers — is the act of hiding or minimizing what you feel in order to appear strong, composed, or in control.

Emotional suppression — especially common among high achievers and trauma survivors — is the act of downplaying or burying emotional responses to maintain control, avoid vulnerability, or project competence.

But suppressing emotion doesn't neutralize it. It stores it. In the body, in the nervous system, and eventually in behaviors that erupt out of proportion. Suppression has a cost: it leaks. Suppressed emotions manifest as chronic stress, anxiety, resentment, physical symptoms, and emotional numbness. Eventually, the body says what the mouth won't.

Staying cool may keep you in control, but it disconnects you from authenticity. People can't connect with your mask — only your truth.

The internalized message is often: *'If I feel it, I'll fall apart. If I express it, I'll be rejected.'* So, people suppress — and suffer. Suppression looks like: forced positivity, sarcasm, intellectualizing, stonewalling, or hyper-productivity.

RESEARCH SPOTLIGHT

Research by Gross & John (2003) found that emotional suppression is associated with poorer interpersonal functioning, less social support, and lower life satisfaction. Over time, chronic suppression is linked to increased sympathetic nervous system arousal and diminished immune response.

A 2009 study published in the *Journal of Personality and Social Psychology* found that individuals who habitually suppressed their emotions experienced fewer positive social outcomes and higher rates of depression over time (Srivastava et al.).

COACH'S INSIGHT

Your body keeps score. What you suppress today becomes tomorrow's resentment, fatigue, or chronic tension. Let it move through — not pile up.

Suppressing emotion isn't self-regulation — it's self-abandonment. And it always collects interest.

CASE STUDY

Derek, an executive coach himself, prided himself on staying calm in conflict. Yet he experienced chronic jaw pain and insomnia. Through somatic coaching, he realized he wasn't calm — he was clenched. Learning to identify and safely express emotions helped his relationships and ended his 2-year sleep struggle.

Exercise 11: Emotional Suppression Inventory (Section 2.6)

Instructions: Reflect on how and when you tend to suppress emotions.

Complete the following prompts:

- I tend to suppress _____ when I feel _____.
- The message I learned growing up about expressing emotion was: _____.
- One cost I've noticed from suppressing is: _____.
- One area where I'd like to express more freely is: _____.

2.7 TEACHING REGULATION IN RELATIONSHIPS: MODELING CALM

Regulation is not just an internal process — it's a relational transmission. You are constantly influencing and being influenced by the nervous systems around you.

Regulation isn't just personal — it's relational. When you model calm, you create emotional safety. When you regulate out loud, you teach others how to do the same.

When you practice emotional regulation in front of others — narrating your experience, owning your emotional state, or taking space intentionally — you become a co-regulator. You model that emotional waves can be surfed, not drowned in.

You don't need to be perfect — just present. Showing your partner, team, or child how you manage frustration or fear builds trust and normalizes emotional complexity.

This is especially important for parents, leaders, and partners. Your ability to remain grounded sets the emotional tone for the room.

Example:

'I'm feeling really activated right now. I'm going to take a minute to breathe so I can show up better.'

This doesn't make you weak. It makes you powerful. Calm is contagious — and so is chaos.

RESEARCH SPOTLIGHT

Attachment theory and polyvagal research demonstrate that co-regulation is crucial for establishing emotional security. According to a 2021 study by Wass and colleagues, dyads who engaged in regulated interactions showed synchronized heart rate variability—a sign of nervous system alignment.

According to psychologist Ed Tronick's 'Still-Face Experiment,' infants and adults alike rely on nonverbal co-regulation for emotional development. Regulated nervous systems create the conditions for relational growth.

COACH'S INSIGHT

You don't need to get it right every time. But when you model how to pause, breathe, and repair, you lead others back to safety. Your presence is more regulating than your perfection. Show people how to recover — not how to pretend.

CASE STUDY

Sophie, a senior partner at a law firm, started narrating her emotional regulation to her team: *'I need to take 2 minutes to reset so I can show up clearly.'* Not only did her team respect her more — they began doing the same, improving the overall tone and collaboration in the firm.

Exercise 12: Co-Regulation Check-In (Section 2.7)

Instructions: Identify one relationship where you'd like to model more emotional regulation.

Reflect:

- What would it sound like to narrate your process aloud?

_____
_____
_____

- What phrases or cues could signal your self-regulation?

_____
_____
_____

- How do you think this might impact the dynamic?

_____
_____
_____
_____

SECTION 3:
COMMUNICATION SKILLS THAT CHANGE EVERYTHING

'The goal of an argument is NOT to win; the goal of an argument is to unpack the conflict towards improved understanding.'
~ Dr. George Vergolias

3.1 WHY WE TALK PAST EACH OTHER: COMMON COMMUNICATION BLOCKS

Miscommunication fuels more conflict than actual disagreement. We assume the other person interprets our words exactly as we meant them. But communication is layered:

- What I meant to say
- What I actually said
- How you interpreted it
- What you felt when you heard it
- What you assumed I meant

When these layers misalign, communication breaks down. The result? People often talk past each other, escalating over misunderstandings rather than genuine disagreements.

This gap causes people to talk past one another. Emotional charge, body language, cultural wiring, and even prior unresolved pain can distort how a message is sent and received.

Common mental blocks:

- Mind reading
- Stonewalling

- Defensiveness
- Tone mismatches
- Competing to be 'right'

We rarely argue about facts — we usually argue about meaning, perception, and unmet needs.

RESEARCH SPOTLIGHT

A study by Tannen (1990) on gender and communication found that up to 70% of conflict in couples stems from style differences in expression and interpretation — not actual disagreement. Well over half of interpersonal conflict arises from differing goals: connection versus control, support versus problem-solving.

COACH'S INSIGHT

Misunderstanding is inevitable. Repair is optional. Great communicators close the gap quickly — not perfectly.

CASE STUDY

Jake and Priya constantly argued about household tasks. Coaching revealed they weren't disagreeing about cleaning — but about feeling appreciated. Once they identified their emotional needs, the arguments nearly disappeared.

Exercise 14: Identify Your Top 3 Communication Blocks (Section 3.1)

Instructions: Reflect on recent conflicts where communication broke down. Use the following questions to explore your patterns:

- Do you tend to shut down, defend, or interrupt?

_____
_____
_____
_____

- What story do you tell yourself in those moments?

  _____
  _____
  _____
  _____

- What communication habits did you inherit from your family or early environment?

  _____
  _____
  _____
  _____

Now write down 3 specific communication blocks that show up often in your relationships.

1. _____
2. _____
3. _____

3.2 ACTIVE LISTENING AS AN ACT OF LEADERSHIP

Listening is a powerful emotional regulator — both for you and the other person. But it's often undervalued.

Listening isn't passive — it's one of the most active things you can do. True listening requires emotional regulation, curiosity, and presence. It builds trust faster than agreement ever will.

In emotionally charged conversations, most people listen to respond — not to understand. Great communicators listen to connect first. Then they validate, then they clarify, then they share. Seek understanding before judgment.

This isn't about losing your voice. It's about making the other person feel safe enough to hear yours.

True listening requires:

- Regulating your own nervous system
- Turning down internal judgment
- Attuning to tone, body language, and unspoken cues

Active listening is not agreement. It's acknowledgment. When someone feels heard, their emotional intensity often softens, making actual communication possible.

The 3-Question Technique to Enhance Communication

The single most impactful technique I have for my coaching clients to improve communication during conflict is a very simple and very effective technique called **'The 3-Question Technique'**. Here's how it works.

You ask 3 simple questions, one at a time.

Question 1: *'Can you teach me your perspective?'*

You then must listen honestly and intently. Your goal is to *understand their perspective* so well that you can share it back to them as well, or even better, than they stated it. The goal here is for understanding ONLY, and NOT for counterpoints or to 'win'. If you feel unclear or unsure about their perspective, you ask clarifying questions TO UNDERSTAND, not to critique or debate. Once you think you understand their perspective, you move on to the second question.

Question 2: Share their perspective as best you can, and then ask,

'Do you think I understand your perspective?' (Or, less formally *'Do you think I understand where you're coming from?'*)

If they agree or say 'yes', you move on to the third question. If they say 'no', or 'sort of' or 'maybe', you continue to ask clarifying questions until you fully understand, and they agree to such. Then move on to the last question.

Question 3: *'Can I teach you my perspective?'*

By this point you have allowed them to feel heard and understood FIRST, and by doing so you have removed their ego from getting in the way or adopting a defensive stance. As a result, they will be much more open to hearing your perspective.

But what if they say *'No, you can't teach me your perspective'* or *'I don't want to hear what you have to say'* or they say, *'F you'* and so on? At that point, you have to move on and come back to the discussion at another time. You don't have an audience! You don't have a willing participant to have an open dialogue. That's ok! At least you demonstrated your ability to listen and to understand first before judgment, and that will set the proper tone for the next time you dialogue. Sometimes people need time to calm down and emotionally regulate prior to being able to have a meaningful dialogue.

The 'I Have A Question' Technique

The **'I have a question'** technique is a conversational strategy that can serve two important purposes.

Imagine you are at a crowded networking event at a conference, and you see several groups of four or five people all standing in circles, talking intently among themselves. You don't know any of them. How do you break into this conversation?

One sure-fire way is to walk up and simply ask, *'Excuse me, I have a question.'* Almost every time they will immediately pause speaking, look at you and ask *'Yes, what's your question?'* It is an amazing way to halt the dialogue and give you an entry point.

Here's the only problem – you have to have a question lined up and ready to go!

While it works wonders at networking events as noted above, in the midst of conflict this technique is designed to make dialogue more constructive, especially in moments of tension, disagreement, or when trying to influence others. Instead of launching into a counterpoint, correction, or critique, you start by framing your input as a genuine question. It can also be used to 'stop the rant' when the person won't give you an opportunity to speak.

For example:

- Instead of: *'That's not how it works.'*
- Try: *'I have a question—how do you see this working if X happens?'*

This subtle shift does three important things:

1. **Lowers defensiveness** — People are less likely to feel attacked when you pose a question instead of making a statement.
2. **Invites collaboration** — It reframes the conversation as mutual problem-solving, not one-sided arguing.
3. **Encourages deeper thinking** — A well-placed question opens space for reflection, allowing others to examine their own assumptions.

4. **Opens curiosity** — by asking the question, it taps into our natural tendency to engage when asked directly, as well as our propensity to want to be helpful.

The 'I have a question' approach is widely associated with Chris Voss, former FBI hostage negotiator, in his book *Never Split the Difference* (2016). Voss emphasizes the power of calibrated questions (e.g., 'How…?' or 'What…?' questions) to guide conversations, defuse tension, and maintain influence without triggering resistance.

The phrasing 'I have a question' became popular in negotiation and leadership communication trainings derived from Voss's work, though the principle itself has roots in Socratic dialogue—using questions to encourage self-examination and collaborative reasoning rather than confrontation.

The BIFF Method

The **BIFF** method is a communication approach that helps shape potentially problematic dialogues towards amicable and productive interactions.

Brief – State your concern briefly and concisely. Don't 'pile on' or give lengthy/wordy explanations, as people tend to numb out or shut down.

Informative – Focus on providing facts and useful information, without digging into the past or bringing up topics or issues that are not part of the current issue at hand.

Friendly – Maintain a friendly, non-judgmental tone. Remember, the goal is not to 'win' an argument, but to create clarity and work towards resolving the conflict.

Firm – You can do all the above AND maintain a respectful tone, while also remaining firm on your needs and non-negotiables.

RESEARCH SPOTLIGHT

Groysberg & Slind (2016) reported in *Harvard Business Review* that 69% of managers say they're uncomfortable communicating with employees. Active listening — especially when feedback is tough — improves team cohesion and reduces turnover.

COACH'S INSIGHT

You can't influence someone who doesn't feel heard. Make listening your leadership superpower.

CASE STUDY

Kara, an executive coach, used active listening during a performance review with a defensive employee. By reflecting back the employee's concerns and slowing her pace, she de-escalated tension and opened space for constructive dialogue.

Danielle, a VP of Marketing, struggled with team morale. By using reflective listening in meetings — paraphrasing and validating — she noticed a 30% increase in engagement scores in under 3 months.

Exercise 15: Reflective Listening Practice (Section 3.2)

Pair up with someone you trust. Take turns sharing a frustration or challenge. The listener should use reflective listening to:

- Paraphrase what they heard
- Validate the emotion
- Ask one open-ended question

Afterward, discuss: How did it feel to be truly listened to? How did it feel to hold back advice and simply reflect?

3.3 SPEAKING SO YOU'RE HEARD: ASSERTIVE VS. AGGRESSIVE VS. PASSIVE

Many people think being direct means being aggressive. Others fear that being honest means being rejected. The truth? Assertive communication is neither aggressive nor passive — it's clear, respectful, and grounded in self-worth.

The ability to assert yourself without overpowering others is a critical conflict skill.

Assertive communication:

- States your needs clearly
- Respects others' boundaries
- Uses 'I' statements
- Avoids blame, contempt, and over-explaining

Aggression uses force. Passivity sacrifices self. Assertion honors both.

- Aggressive = 'I matter, you don't.'
- Passive = 'You matter, I don't.'
- Assertive = 'We both matter.'

Assertiveness is not about tone — it's about intention. It means owning your truth without apology and delivering it with dignity.

And it's a practice — not a personality trait.

RESEARCH SPOTLIGHT

A meta-analysis by Wilson & Gallois (1993) found that assertive communication was significantly correlated with better psychological well-being, interpersonal effectiveness, and leadership ratings across diverse workplace settings.

COACH'S INSIGHT

Clarity is not cruelty. You don't have to choose between being kind and being clear — true assertiveness is both.

CASE STUDY

Marcos, a product manager, avoided conflict by sugarcoating feedback. Once he learned to use assertive I' statements — e.g., *I feel stuck when projects are delayed without communication* — team productivity and trust improved dramatically.

Exercise 16: Finding Your Assertive Voice (Section 3.3)

Objective:
To practice shifting from passive or aggressive communication to confident, assertive dialogue.

Instructions:

1. **Recall a Recent Conversation That Didn't Go Well**
   - What was the topic?
   - How did you express yourself? (e.g., did you shut down, get loud, avoid the topic?)
   - How did the other person respond?

Write 2–3 sentences summarizing it:

_____
_____
_____

2. **Label Your Style**
   How was your communication style in that moment:
   - Passive
   - Aggressive
   - Passive-aggressive
   - Assertive

   Why did you choose that answer?

   _____
   _____
   _____
   _____

3. **Reframe It Assertively**
   Now, rewrite what you *wish* you had said — using an assertive tone. Focus on 'I' statements, clarity, and respect.

   Example: 'I felt dismissed when my ideas weren't acknowledged. Can we find a way to make sure everyone gets heard?'

   Your new script:

   _____
   _____
   _____
   _____

Coach's Challenge:
Say this script out loud in front of a mirror or record yourself.

- What felt strong?
- What felt awkward or forced?
- What's one word you want to practice using more often in difficult conversations?

Exercise 17 : Practicing Assertiveness (Chapter 3.3)

Instructions: Think of a situation where you were either too passive or too aggressive in communication.

1. Describe the situation briefly:

_____
_____

2. What did you say or do in the moment?

_____
_____

3. What would an assertive version of that response sound like?

_____
_____
_____

Use 'I' statements and clear, respectful language.

- Example: 'I feel frustrated when meetings start late because it makes me feel like my time isn't valued.'

Write your assertive version:

_____
_____

3.4 THE POWER OF LANGUAGE: FRAMING AND REFRAMING

Words shape reality. In conflict, the way something is said often matters more than what is said. How you frame a conflict can entrench a power struggle — or create a path to resolution.

Framing sets tone. Reframing changes lens.

> Framing = how you present information
> Reframing = how you shift interpretation

Example:

- Blame frame: 'You never listen.'
- Reframe: 'I feel unheard and want to connect more clearly.'

Try shifting from:

- 'You're wrong' →   'Help me understand your view.'
- 'You always do this' →   'This pattern is hard for me.'
- 'This won't work' →   'What would make this feel possible?'

This isn't about sugarcoating. It's about effectiveness. Blame makes people defensive. Framing invites dialogue.

Reframing doesn't erase the problem — it reorients you toward possibility.

RESEARCH SPOTLIGHT

Cognitive reframing, as studied in CBT research (Beck, 1979), has been shown to significantly reduce emotional reactivity and increase communication satisfaction in high-conflict couples.

COACH'S INSIGHT

Reframing isn't denial — it's redesign. When you change the frame, you shift the story you're stuck in.

CASE STUDY

Ari and Sam had recurring fights about finances. When they reframed their arguments as 'a shared challenge' rather than 'a personal failing,' they began budgeting collaboratively instead of blaming reactively.

Exercise 18: Reframing Language (Section 3.4)

Instructions: Take 3 common blame-based phrases you catch yourself saying and reframe them with ownership and collaboration in mind.

Examples:

- Blame: 'You never help around the house.' → Reframe: 'I feel overwhelmed and would love to share the load more evenly.'
- Blame: 'You don't care about my feelings.' → Reframe: 'When I'm upset and don't get a response, I feel invisible.'

Now write your own:

- Blame:_____ → Reframe:_____
- Blame:_____ → Reframe:_____

3.5. REPAIR LANGUAGE: WHAT TO SAY AFTER A BLOW-UP

Every relationship hits a rupture. What matters most is whether you know how to repair.

Repair is the sacred reset. Without it, conflict cycles repeat.

Repair doesn't require you to be wrong — it requires you to be responsible.

Elements of effective repair:

- Acknowledge impact
- Take responsibility (even partial)
- Invite dialogue
- Reconnect intentionally

Powerful repair language includes:

- *'I see how that hurt you.'*
- *'I want to understand better — can we revisit this?'*
- *'I handled that poorly. Can I try again?'*

What's needed most after conflict is acknowledgment, not perfection. Rupture is inevitable. Repair is a skill — and a signal of emotional maturity.

RESEARCH SPOTLIGHT

John Gottman's research (1999) found that couples who engage in regular repair attempts — even imperfect ones — are significantly more likely to stay together long-term, regardless of how often they argue.

COACH'S INSIGHT

You don't need a script — you need sincerity. Repair starts with ownership and ends with re-connection.

CASE STUDY

After a heated exchange in a boardroom, Priya followed up with her colleague the next day and said: *'I regret how I handled that. Let's reset.'* Her vulnerability turned a near fallout into a strengthened alliance.

Exercise 19: Build Your Repair Toolkit (Section 3.5)

Objective:
To practice the art of repair — the most powerful tool for rebuilding trust after conflict.

Instructions:

1. **Reflect on a Rupture**
   Think of a time when you hurt someone — or were hurt — and the issue was left unresolved.

   What happened? _____

   How do you think the other person felt? _____

2. **Name the Impact & Own Your Role**
   Even if you weren't 'wrong,' take responsibility for your impact. Write 1–2 sentences below.

   Example: 'I see now that I shut you down when I rolled my eyes. That wasn't fair.'

   _____
   _____
   _____
   _____

3. **Write Your Repair Statement**
   Now create a short statement to invite reconnection. Use empathy + ownership.
   Examples:

   - 'I want to understand what that felt like for you.'
   - 'That wasn't my best moment — and I care about how it landed.'
   - 'Can we start fresh and talk through this again?'

   _____
   _____
   _____
   _____

4. **Optional Step — Deliver It**
   If appropriate, try delivering your repair statement. Reflect afterward:

   - How did it feel? _____
   - How was it received? _____
   - What would you do differently next time? _____

SECTION 4:
THE V.E.N.T. METHOD IN ACTION

'Be curious, not judgmental.'
~ Ted Lasso

4.1 OVERVIEW OF THE V.E.N.T. METHOD™

The V.E.N.T. Method is an approach to conflict resolution that I developed based on years of experience as a forensic psychologist and executive coach, working in high-pressure and high-stakes situations, including prisons, law enforcement consultations, hostage situations, active shooter threats, and emergency departments.

It offers a powerful, repeatable framework for de-escalating and resolving conflicts in real-time. The V.E.N.T. Method™ is a clinically informed, easy-to-remember conflict resolution model designed to help people stay emotionally grounded and relationally effective when conversations get tense. Whether you're navigating a difficult discussion with a partner, colleague, or family member, this model gives you a reliable map:

- V = Validate the Emotion
- E = Engage Curiously
- N = Navigate Needs
- T = Transform the Pattern

V.E.N.T. is more than a technique. It's a mindset shift — away from blame and reactivity, toward emotional literacy, empathy, and solution-focused action.

4.2 V = VALIDATE: THE FIRST DE-ESCALATION TOOL

Validation is the single most powerful way to de-escalate a conflict. When people feel seen and heard, they calm down. When they feel dismissed, they escalate.

Validation is not the same as agreeing or condoning. It simply means acknowledging the emotional experience of the other person:

- 'That makes sense given what you're going through.'
- 'I can understand why that would be frustrating.'
- 'That sounds really frustrating.'
- 'I can see why you'd feel that way.'

Even subtle invalidation *'You're overreacting'*, or *'That's not what I meant'*) triggers defensiveness. Validation is the off-ramp from that cycle.

4.3 E = ENGAGE CURIOUSLY: ASK, DON'T ACCUSE

Curiosity disarms defensiveness. Curious questions invite exploration, not interrogation. Rather than assuming motives or jumping to conclusions, curious engagement invites understanding:

- 'Can you walk me through what you were feeling?'
- 'What part of this hit the hardest for you?'
- 'Can you tell me more about that?'
- 'What's the hardest part of this for you?'
- 'What do you need most right now?'

This step turns conflict into collaboration. The tone matters — genuine curiosity, not interrogation. Avoid rapid-fire or loaded questions.

When people are given space to speak without fear of being judged, they tend to soften and clarify. That's where insight lives.

4.4 N = NAVIGATE NEEDS: UNSPOKEN NEEDS FUEL ONGOING CONFLICT

Most recurring arguments are symptoms — not root causes. Beneath the surface of conflict are unmet wants and needs:

- To feel respected

- To feel in control
- To feel loved or valued
- To feel safe

By identifying and naming the unmet need — both yours and theirs — you remove ambiguity and can collaborate on solutions.

Identify your needs, then ask:

- 'What am I really needing right now?'
- 'What might they be needing that I'm not seeing?'
- What are my needs vs. my wants vs my non-negotiables?
- 'I think what I'm really needing here is reassurance.'
- 'Do you think what you're needing is more follow-through from me?'

Needs are not selfish. They're the language of emotional reality.

4.5 T = TRANSFORM: REPAIR THE PATTERN, DON'T REPEAT IT

The final step is action. Transforming a rupture means consciously shifting away from reactive habits and toward new patterns.

Repeating ingrained patterns can become a default mechanism and a way to avoid uncomfortable emotions. Repairing patterns build trust.

The difference?

Repeating hides problems that need attention.

Repairing heals what needs healing!

Transformation might sound like:

- 'Let's reset and try this again, slower.'
- 'I'll take more ownership next time — let's make a plan that works for both of us.'

You're not aiming for perfect resolution. You're aiming for progress, trust, and repair. That's what transforms a reactive loop into a growth experience.

4.6 WHEN V.E.N.T. DOESN'T WORK — SIGNS OF DEEPER ISSUES

While the V.E.N.T. Method™ is highly effective, it isn't a cure-all. If a conversation keeps breaking down, look for deeper issues such as:

- High-conflict personalities (e.g., narcissism, untreated trauma)
- Safety concerns (verbal or emotional abuse)
- Repeated invalidation or stonewalling
- Past wounds that haven't been processed

In such cases, resolution may require therapy, structured mediation, or setting boundaries — not just improved communication tools.

Most conflict is like repairing a flat tire. When we get a flat tire, we never walk back down the road to dig up the past and see what caused it – instead, we focus on the problem at hand, how to repair or replace the tire, and get back on the road.

Yet, if we repeatedly get a flat tire, then we must dig a bit deeper into what is causing this to recur.

4.7 PRACTICING THE MODEL WITH REAL SCRIPTS + SCENARIOS

Scenario 1: Your coworker interrupts you in a meeting.

- Validate: 'I can see you were eager to contribute — I value that.'
- Engage: 'Can we talk about how to make space for both of us to share?'
- Navigate: 'What I'm needing is space to finish my thought before feedback.'
- Transform: 'Let's set a norm in our team to signal when we want to jump in.'

Scenario 2: Your partner is upset about how you handled a social event.

- Validate: 'You're right — I didn't loop you in, and that felt hurtful.'
- Engage: 'What did that bring up for you emotionally?'
- Navigate: 'I think I was trying to avoid tension, but I see that didn't help.'
- Transform: 'Next time, I'll check in with you first. Let's plan that together.'

Scenario 3: Your partner says you never listen.

- Validate: 'I can see why you'd feel unheard when I interrupt.'
- Engage: 'What part of what I said made it feel that way?'
- Navigate: 'I think what I really want is to feel respected too.'
- Transform: 'Let's try again. I'll listen fully and then respond.'

4.8 REAL-LIFE CONFLICT RESOLUTION DIALOGUES + TECHNIQUE BREAKDOWNS

Scenario 1: Romantic Relationship — Feeling Unheard

Context: Jamie feels like their partner Taylor never really listens during conversations about household responsibilities.

> Dialogue:
> Jamie: *'I feel like you're not really hearing me when I talk about how stressed I am.'*
> Taylor: *'That's not fair — I do listen.'*
>
> Jamie: *'Okay, I hear that. But it feels like when I bring things up, you either shut down or change the subject.'*
> Taylor: (pauses) *'I can see why you'd feel that way. I probably do that when I feel criticized.'*
>
> Jamie: *'That makes sense. What do you need in those moments so we can talk without it escalating?'*
> Taylor: *'Maybe just a heads-up when it's serious. That would help me stay open instead of defensive.'*
>
> Jamie: *'Let's try that. I'll flag when I need us to focus, and we'll both slow down.'*

Techniques Used:

- V = Validate: 'I can see why you'd feel that way.'
- E = Engage Curiously: 'What do you need in those moments...'
- N = Navigate Needs: Identified the need for advance notice and emotional preparation.
- T = Transform: Collaborative plan to improve future conversations.

Scenario 2: Workplace — Feeling Overlooked in Meetings

Context: Malik feels like his manager, Sarah, keeps cutting him off in team meetings.

>Dialogue:
>Malik: *'Sarah, I wanted to check in about something that's been bothering me.'*
>Sarah: *'Sure, what's going on?'*
>
>Malik: *'In a few of our meetings, I've noticed I get interrupted or redirected mid-sentence. It leaves me feeling like my input doesn't matter.'*
>Sarah: *'Oh, wow. I didn't realize I was doing that.'*
>
>Malik: *'I know it may not be intentional. I just wanted to share because it's impacting how I show up.'*
>Sarah: *'Thanks for telling me. I can work on making space. Do you want to lead off the next meeting to set the tone?'*
>
>Malik: *'I'd appreciate that. Let's give it a shot.'*

Techniques Used:

- Assertive Communication: 'It leaves me feeling like my input doesn't matter.'

- Reframing: Emphasized impact over blame.

- V.E.N.T. Application:

    - V: Validation — Sarah acknowledged and appreciated the feedback.

    - E: Engaged curiously — stayed open to the conversation.

    - N: Identified need for visibility and respect.

    - T: Concrete action — leading the next meeting.

Scenario 3: Friendship — Canceling Plans Repeatedly

Context: Ildiko feels like her friend Jenna has been canceling plans too often and it's starting to hurt.

>Dialogue:
>Ildiko: *'Hey, can we talk about something a little awkward?'*
>Jenna: *'Of course, what's up?'*

Ildiko: *'I've noticed a pattern where we make plans and then they get canceled. It's starting to feel like I'm not a priority.'*

Jenna: *'Oh no — I didn't mean for it to come off that way. Things have been chaotic with work.'*

Ildiko: *'I get that. And I'm not mad, just feeling disappointed. Our hangouts mean a lot to me.'*

Jenna: *'I'm glad you told me. Let's block a few dates this month — I'll treat it like a real commitment.'*

Ildiko: *'Thanks. That helps me feel more valued.'*

Techniques Used:

- Naming the Pattern: 'I've noticed a pattern . . .'
- Emotional Honesty Without Blame: 'It's starting to feel like I'm not a priority.'
- Validation & Empathy: Jenna acknowledged the disappointment and gave context.
- Collaborative Repair: Future plans were agreed upon with mutual intention.

4.9 CORE NEEDS INVENTORY – WORKSHEET

Use this worksheet to identify the core emotional needs that surface most often during conflict. Mark the needs that resonate with you and reflect using the journal prompts provided.

STEP 1: Identify Your Needs

Place a checkmark next to the needs that are frequently activated for you in conflict. Then, circle your top 3.

- ☐ To feel heard
- ☐ To feel understood
- ☐ To feel respected
- ☐ To feel emotionally safe
- ☐ To feel appreciated
- ☐ To feel autonomy / freedom
- ☐ To feel trusted
- ☐ To feel supported
- ☐ To feel connected
- ☐ To feel loved
- ☐ To feel included / not left out
- ☐ To feel competent
- ☐ To feel prioritized
- ☐ To feel secure / not abandoned
- ☐ To feel validated
- ☐ To feel seen / acknowledged
- ☐ To feel fair treatment / justice
- ☐ To feel physical safety
- ☐ To feel control or influence
- ☐ To feel intimacy or closeness

STEP 2: Reflect & Journal

Answer the following prompts to deepen your awareness of your core needs:

1. Which three needs get most activated when you conflict with someone you care about?

___

2. What happens internally (emotionally or physically) when those needs feel unmet?

___

3. Are these needs familiar from earlier in your life — childhood, family, or past relationships?

___

4. How can you express these needs assertively without blame?

___

5. What would it look like to help the other person feel their core need is being met too?

___

Exercise 20: V.E.N.T. Self-Reflection (Section 4)

Choose a recent conflict and reflect:

- VALIDATE: What could you have said to make the other person feel heard?
- ENGAGE: What curious questions did you ask — or could have asked?
- NAVIGATE: What unspoken needs were fueling your emotional response?
- TRANSFORM: What new action/repair statement would move the relationship forward?

Write a sample V.E.N.T. statement you could have used:

- Validate: _____
- Engage: _____
- Navigate: _____
- Transform: _____

NOTES & REFLECTIONS

Use this space to reflect on how you've used V.E.N.T. in real interactions and what shifted as a result.

Exercise 21: Reflective Journal Prompts (Section 4)

1. When someone challenges me, do I listen to connect or listen to defend?

_____
_____
_____
_____

2. What tone or word choice triggers defensiveness in me — and why?

_____
_____
_____
_____

3. What's the difference between being honest and being hurtful?

_____
_____
_____
_____

4. How did my family handle conflict — and how does that show up in my relationships today?

_____
_____
_____
_____

5. What's one conflict I could revisit using the V.E.N.T. method that might shift the outcome?

_____
_____
_____
_____

SECTION 5:
BOUNDARIES THAT ACTUALLY WORK

'Your destiny is determined by the choices you make.'
~ Tony Robbins

5.1 WHAT BOUNDARIES REALLY ARE (AND AREN'T)

Boundaries aren't about controlling others — they're about clearly defining what we are and are not available for.

Boundaries are essential tools for protecting our emotional well-being, not mechanisms for controlling other people. When we think of boundaries as rules for others to follow, we get trapped in power struggles. They clarify responsibility, protect emotional energy, and establish personal sovereignty.

Boundaries are not ultimatums. They are not punishments. They are not rigid rules imposed on others. They are proactive expressions of self-respect.

And when we understand them as commitments to ourselves, the dynamic shifts entirely.

A healthy boundary sounds like: *'I don't take work calls after 7 p.m.'* or *'If yelling continues, I will leave the conversation.'* Notice: these statements are not demands for the other person to behave differently. They are clear, enforceable actions we take based on our own values.

We often confuse boundaries with barriers. But boundaries are bridges — they allow us to stay in relationship without self-betrayal.

If you feel guilt or resistance when considering a boundary, ask: *'Am I choosing discomfort now in the service of long-term self-respect?'*

COACH'S INSIGHT

When clients say, *'setting boundaries didn't work,'* they usually mean the other person didn't like it. Your boundary is still valid — even if it's challenged or ignored.

RESEARCH SPOTLIGHT

A 2021 study in the *Journal of Social and Personal Relationships* found that individuals with clear personal boundaries report higher relationship satisfaction and lower emotional burnout.

CASE STUDY

Anna often agreed to family events she didn't want to attend. When she started saying no, her relatives called her selfish. She held firm and later reported feeling more peaceful and less resentful. Eventually, her family adjusted.

Exercise 22:   Reframing Unhealthy Boundaries (Section 5.1)

Exercise: Defining Your Boundaries

Think of a relationship or recurring situation where you feel drained or frustrated.

Step 1: Describe what's happening

_____

_____

_____

_____

Step 2: Now reframe that situation with a healthy boundary you'd like to set.

(Example: Instead of tolerating disrespectful jokes, you might say: 'I'm not okay with those comments and will walk away if they continue.')

_____

_____

_____

_____

5.2 WHY MOST PEOPLE STRUGGLE TO SET BOUNDARIES

People struggle with boundaries not because they don't know what they need — but because they fear the cost of enforcing them. Fear of conflict, rejection, abandonment, or guilt often keeps us silent. But silence costs us far more in the long run. We trade peace for people-pleasing and self-betrayal.

The resistance to boundary-setting is almost always emotional, not logistical. We don't avoid them because we don't know what to say — we avoid them because we anticipate relational fallout. We've been trained to believe that prioritizing ourselves is selfish, especially if we've grown up in families where self-sacrifice was the norm.

For many high-achieving professionals, boundaries feel like weakness or laziness. But burnout isn't a badge of honor — it's a signal that something internal needs attention. If you find yourself justifying boundary violations with phrases like 'it's just this once' or 'they're going through a lot,' ask yourself: what pattern am I reinforcing?

You don't need to justify your limits. Clear is kind. Unclear is unkind — to yourself and others.

COACH'S INSIGHT

Boundaries will make some people uncomfortable — especially those who benefited from your lack of them.

RESEARCH SPOTLIGHT

Studies on attachment, such as that by Mikulincer & Shaver (2007) show that those with anxious styles often override their own boundaries to avoid perceived rejection.

CASE STUDY

Dev always stayed late to cover for his manager. When he started leaving on time, he was labeled 'unreliable.' Yet his productivity improved, and he secured a new role in a healthier environment.

Exercise 23: Confronting the Resistance to Set Boundaries (Section 5.2)

List 3 reasons why you hesitate to set boundaries with certain people.

1. _____
2. _____
3. _____

Now challenge each reason.

Ask: Is this fear a real or inherited one? Is the cost of discomfort worth the long-term peace?

1. _____
2. _____
3. _____

5.3 INTERNAL VS. EXTERNAL BOUNDARIES

External boundaries are what we say or do to define our limits with others.

Internal boundaries are the limits we set with ourselves — on our time, self-talk, energy, or reactivity.

Said another way, external boundaries define how we expect to be treated by others. Internal boundaries define how we manage ourselves. Without internal boundaries, even external ones collapse. We become reactive instead of intentional.

Most people focus on the external — what others are doing wrong — without realizing their internal boundary is leaking.

If I keep engaging in the same argument expecting a different result, that's an internal boundary issue. If I replay the conversation on a loop all night, that's an internal boundary issue. If I agree to something I don't want and then act passive-aggressively, that's an internal boundary issue.

Internal boundaries are the foundation of emotional self-regulation. They include:

- Saying no to self-criticism
- Creating space before reacting
- Enforcing limits around digital overwhelm

When you build strong internal boundaries, your external ones become easier to communicate and enforce — not from anger, but clarity.

COACH'S INSIGHT

If you keep setting boundaries with someone who ignores them — your next boundary is with yourself: stop participating in the cycle.

RESEARCH SPOTLIGHT

Dr. Brené Brown in her pivotal book *Daring Greatly* (2012) defines boundaries as 'what's okay and what's not okay,' and ties them directly to compassion, not disconnection.

CASE STUDY

Tasha vowed not to check work email after 7 p.m. But without reinforcing that with herself, she kept breaking the rule. After setting a nightly alarm and deleting Slack from her phone, she finally reclaimed her evenings.

Exercise 24:   Build Internal Boundaries First (Section 5.3)

Choose one internal boundary to practice this week:

- No phone after 9 p.m.
- Limit self-criticism using a mantra like: *'I'm doing my best right now.'*
- Take 3 deep breaths before responding to any triggering comment.

Track your progress and emotional response over 7 days.

5.4 THE CONSEQUENCES OF LEAKY AND RIGID BOUNDARIES

Leaky boundaries look like people-pleasing, burnout, and resentment. Leaky boundaries are boundaries we set but don't enforce. Rigid boundaries look like avoidance, walls, and disconnection. Rigid boundaries are inflexible walls designed to keep people out.

Both extremes come from fear — fear of conflict or fear of vulnerability.

When boundaries are leaky, we over-function. We say yes too quickly, absorb others' emotional burdens, or allow disrespectful behavior without consequence. The result? Chronic resentment, burnout, and relationship fatigue.

When boundaries are rigid, we under-function relationally. We may shut down, ghost, or emotionally withdraw to avoid discomfort. This might feel protective in the short term, but over time it leads to isolation and unprocessed conflict.

Healthy boundaries are flexible — they adapt, but don't collapse. They change depending on context, history, and intention — but they are always grounded in self-respect.

You can be both compassionate and clear. You can say no and still care deeply.

Ask yourself: Do I lean toward leaky or rigid boundaries? How do I want to recalibrate?

COACH'S INSIGHT

If you feel resentful, depleted, or taken for granted — you don't need more generosity. You need more boundaries.

RESEARCH SPOTLIGHT

Buehler and colleagues, in the *Journal of Child Development* (2007) found that adolescents in families with healthy boundaries had greater psychological well-being, emotional regulation, and relationship stability.

CASE STUDY

Mark responded to every after-hours email from his team. He thought it showed commitment. Instead, it trained his team to expect 24/7 access. When he finally drew the line, the pushback was short-lived — and his stress level dropped within a week.

Exercise 25: Recalibrate Your Boundary Style (Section 5.4)

Draw a line with two ends labeled 'LEAKY' and 'RIGID'. Place yourself where you tend to fall most often.

Leaky ←——————————————→ Rigid

- Think of one relationship you want to adjust your boundaries in.

_____
_____
_____

- Write out a revised boundary using clear, compassionate language

    Example: 'I love spending time with you, and I also need one night a week to recharge alone.'

_____
_____

Exercise 26: Reflective Journal Prompts (Section 5):

- What messages did you receive growing up about boundaries?

- Do you see boundaries as selfish or empowering?

- How would your life change if you honored your limits without guilt?

- Who in your life makes it hardest to set boundaries?

- What are you afraid will happen if you assert yourself?

- What has actually happened in the past when you've tried?

- Where do your internal boundaries tend to collapse first — time, energy, thoughts?

- What helps you feel emotionally regulated and grounded?

- What agreements can you make with yourself today?

- What emotion most often drives your boundary patterns — fear, guilt, anger, shame?

- What would 'flexible clarity' look like for you in one important relationship?

SECTION 6:
CONFLICT IN DIFFERENT RELATIONSHIPS

'That's what you do when you're angry with someone, you keep them a part of your life.'
~ Garrison Keillor

6.1 CONFLICT IN ROMANTIC RELATIONSHIPS: ATTACHMENT AND INTIMACY

Romantic conflict is rarely about logistics—it's about emotional safety. Romantic relationships stir up the deepest parts of us—our longings, fears, and attachment wounds.

Beneath the surface of nearly every fight is a fear of disconnection, abandonment, or not being fully seen. The dishes, the calendar, the tone of voice—these are just proxies for deeper attachment wounds. Conflict here often isn't about 'the thing'—it's about what the thing symbolizes.

Partners bring their attachment styles into the relationship: anxious partners may pursue conflict with intensity, while avoidant partners may shut down.

When one partner feels dismissed, it may trigger an old fear of abandonment. When the other feels blamed, it may ignite shame or inadequacy. Unless we recognize these patterns, we play them out instead of working through them.

These dynamics collide under stress, creating cycles of protest and withdrawal.

COACH'S INSIGHT

When couples learn to separate their attachment wounds from the current moment, conflict transforms. One client said, *'I realized I wasn't mad at my partner—I was terrified they'd leave like my dad did.'* That clarity changed everything.

I tell clients: don't fight the fight—decode it. One couple kept arguing about who planned more date nights. We uncovered that one partner was desperate to feel chosen, while the other feared rejection for 'getting it wrong.' Naming that transformed the dialogue.

RESEARCH SPOTLIGHT

Attachment theory shows that secure partners are more likely to approach conflict with openness, while anxious or avoidant styles tend to escalate or shut down (Mikulincer & Shaver, 2016).

According to Dr. Sue Johnson (Emotionally Focused Therapy), 70% of relationship conflict is rooted in unmet attachment needs—like needing to feel secure, valued, or emotionally accessible.

CASE STUDY

A couple came to coaching, constantly arguing over 'who does more.' We uncovered that the real issue wasn't dishes or calendars—it was a cry for appreciation and fear of invisibility. Once named, the fights subsided dramatically.

A couple on the brink of separation reframed their fights using the V.E.N.T. Method™. Instead of saying, *'You never listen'*, they practiced, *'I feel anxious when I can't reach you. I need to feel like I matter.'* Their entire emotional climate shifted.

Exercise 27: Attachment Awareness Map (Section 6.1)

- Attachment Awareness Map: Identify your attachment style (secure, anxious, avoidant) using a validated quiz, such as the one you can find here: https://attachment.personal-developmentschool.com

    Reflect on how this shows up in your conflicts.

- Rewrite the Script: Think of a recent fight. Rewrite it using the V.E.N.T. Method™, focusing on naming the emotion, engaging with curiosity, and identifying needs.

- Journal Prompt: What patterns from your family of origin show up most in your romantic conflicts?

_____

_____

6.2 CONFLICT DURING SEPARATION & DIVORCE: THE RULES CHANGE

In divorce, conflict enters a new phase. You're no longer arguing to resolve a shared future—you're negotiating separation. Roles dissolve, and power struggles spike. Old triggers intensify. Grief masquerades as rage. Co-parenting becomes a pressure cooker.

Conflict during separation and divorce has higher emotional stakes—and less clear rules. Co-parenting, legal agreements, and grief collide in messy ways. The emotional brain hijacks logic. Even well-meaning people weaponize communication when feeling betrayed or discarded. The key is to shift from fighting your ex to protecting your peace.

(For a deeper dive into navigating conflict during separation and divorce, check out Section 10!)

COACH'S INSIGHT

Trying to win the breakup often costs you your peace. I remind clients: you're not just ending a relationship—you're writing the postscript. Write one that honors your integrity.

In high-stakes transitions like divorce, you need an internal compass. One client reframed his role from 'vindicated ex' to 'co-parent with integrity.' That clarity changed how he showed up in every interaction. How we re-invent ourselves and our roles determines how we show up, which in turn determines whether the outcome moves towards conflict or peace.

RESEARCH SPOTLIGHT

High-conflict divorces are associated with long-term psychological effects on children—more than the divorce itself (Kelly & Emery, 2003).

High-conflict divorce is associated with long-term psychological effects on children—including anxiety, loyalty conflicts, and impaired emotional regulation (Amato & Afifi, 2006).

CASE STUDY

One man I coached reframed his goal from 'getting even' to 'modeling emotional responsibility for my daughter.' His ex stopped fighting him. He stopped fighting himself.

A divorcing mother was triggered by her ex's new partner. Instead of reacting, she journaled, focusing on clearly naming her current emotional needs. Her real need? To feel respected as a parent. That clarity helped her set boundaries with confidence and without emotional landmines.

Exercise 28: Your Boundary Blueprint & Co-Parenting Comms Plan (Section 6.2)

- Boundary Blueprint: List 3 non-negotiable boundaries you need to protect your peace during this transition.

1. _____
2. _____
3. _____

- Co-Parenting Communication Plan: Draft a neutral, concise message about a recent parenting issue—remove judgment and keep it fact-based.

_____
_____
_____
_____

- Journal Prompt: What's one way you can model emotional responsibility for your children (or yourself) this week?

_____
_____
_____
_____

6.3 FRIENDSHIP CONFLICTS: BETRAYAL, GHOSTING, AND MISMATCHED EXPECTATIONS

Friendship conflict often catches people off guard, and it is often minimized—but it cuts deep. Unlike romantic or family roles, friendship boundaries are often unwritten. That ambiguity leads to unmet needs and silent resentments. Because we don't formally define these relationships, we assume alignment—until it breaks.

Friendship ruptures often involve mismatched expectations around time, emotional availability, or unspoken resentment. Unlike romantic or familial ties, people often ghost instead of repair, leading to unresolved grief.

COACH'S INSIGHT

Ghosting doesn't always mean malice—it often signals overwhelm, conflict avoidance, or mismatched expectations. But your hurt is still valid.

Not all friendships are meant to last forever. But every rupture is an invitation to understand your boundaries, expectations, and patterns.

RESEARCH SPOTLIGHT

Friendship dissolution is linked to increased loneliness, rumination, and identity disruption (Adams & Blieszner, 1995). Yet, people rarely seek support around it.

Studies show that unresolved friendship losses cause as much psychological distress as romantic breakups (Fehr, 2000). Yet these events are often minimized in society.

CASE STUDY

A client ghosted a friend after feeling disrespected. Through coaching, he initiated a direct conversation that clarified both sides. The friendship didn't survive—but his self-respect did.

A client felt devastated after being ghosted by a friend of 15 years. In coaching, she processed the grief, named her core need for closure, and sent a message not for reconciliation, but for release. Her anxiety lifted almost instantly.

Exercise 29: The Friendship Audit & Closure Letter (Section 6.3)

- Friendship Audit:
  List your top five friendships. Note which feel reciprocal, which feel draining, and why.

1. _____
2. _____
3. _____
4. _____
5. _____

- Closure Letter: Write (but don't send) a letter to a friend where there's unresolved tension. State your feelings and needs clearly. This letter is for you, to help you clarify, bring awareness to, and express your feelings.

- Journal Prompt: How do you want to feel in your closest friendships, and what boundaries would support that?

_____
_____
_____
_____

6.4 WORK CONFLICTS: POWER, POLITICS, AND PSYCHOLOGICAL SAFETY

Conflict at work isn't just about tasks—it's about power, visibility, and identity. Workplace conflict is less personal—but no less emotional. Hierarchies, turf wars, unclear expectations, and psychological safety all play a role.

The mistake many professionals make? Treating interpersonal issues as purely strategic problems. But conflict at work, like anywhere else, is deeply human.

Leaders often suppress tension to keep the peace, but unresolved workplace conflict festers, fueling disengagement and turnover.

Workplace culture either supports open dialogue or punishes it. Psychological safety is key: if people fear retaliation or embarrassment, they won't speak up—even when it matters most.

COACH'S INSIGHT

Conflict resilience is a leadership skill. You can be kind and still be direct. You can disagree without disrespect. And you can repair without losing credibility.

Conflict fluency is a leadership advantage. One executive shifted from defensiveness to curiosity during performance reviews. Result? Better morale, more innovation, and stronger retention.

RESEARCH SPOTLIGHT

In a study conducted by Rozovsky using Google's Project Aristotle, they found that psychological safety—not raw intelligence—was the #1 predictor of team performance. Teams that address tension early outperform those that avoid it. (Google's Project Aristotle, 2016)

CASE STUDY

A C-suite executive used the V.E.N.T. Method™ to address a direct report's passive aggression. The result? Not just improved communication, but renewed trust—and a ripple effect across the team.

A mid-level manager feared confronting a toxic peer. With scripting and rehearsal, she initiated a boundary-setting conversation using the V.E.N.T. framework. Tension decreased, and other team members began speaking up, too.

Exercise 30: Conflict Role-Play & Conflict Power Mapping (Section 6.4)

- Conflict Role-Play: Script a difficult work conversation using assertive, non-accusatory language. Practice it aloud, preferably in front of a mirror.

- Power Mapping: Identify stakeholders in your conflict and their likely motivations. Consider how that shapes your strategy.

- Journal Prompt: When have you avoided a work conflict out of fear, and what did it cost you?

6.5 SOCIAL MEDIA, DIGITAL CONFLICT, AND 'PERFORMATIVE OUTRAGE'

Digital conflict is fast, public, and often cruel. Conflict now plays out in comment threads, group chats, and subtweets. Social media fuels binary thinking, outrage culture, and depersonalized attacks.

In digital spaces, we often forget there's a human behind the screen—and conflict becomes performance, not conversation. Online, people are more likely to project, polarize, and punish. Conflict becomes performance—designed to signal identity or loyalty, not resolve disagreement.

The lack of facial cues, tone, and real-time feedback reduces empathy. Small disagreements escalate. Nuance dies in the algorithm. It is a perfect environment for keyboard warriors who struggle with handling conflict directly and adaptively.

COACH'S INSIGHT

Before you respond online, ask: Am I trying to connect—or to dominate? Am I engaging or performing? Those questions alone can change your tone.

Before you post, ask: Am I trying to express, or trying to explode? One client said, 'I stopped treating every post like a courtroom.' That shift restored his digital peace.

RESEARCH SPOTLIGHT

The 'online disinhibition effect' shows people behave with less empathy and more aggression online due to perceived anonymity and detachment (Suler, 2004). Digital conflict increases emotional intensity while reducing empathy and resolution outcomes.

CASE STUDY

A client almost lost a job over a reactive post. In coaching, we reframed his digital communication as an extension of his values—not his venting. He now leads leadership change discussions—with nuance and impact.

A client publicly clapped back at a colleague's post—and regretted it immediately. In coaching, we unpacked the emotional trigger and developed a digital boundary plan. He later repaired the relationship offline.

Exercise 31: Your Digital Delay Rule & Trigger Mapping (Section 6.5)

- Digital Delay Rule: Commit to a 24-hour delay before posting or replying to emotionally charged content. Track your results for one week.

- Trigger Mapping: List three social media topics or accounts that reliably provoke you. Identify the underlying emotional trigger.

1. _____ Trigger: _____
2. _____ Trigger: _____
3. _____ Trigger: _____

- Journal Prompt: How can you use your digital presence to connect rather than perform?

_____
_____
_____
_____

6.6 GENDER, IDENTITY & EMOTIONAL LABOR IN CONFLICT DYNAMICS

Conflict doesn't occur in a vacuum. Not everyone is allowed to express anger the same way. Gender roles, race, class, and neurodiversity all shape how conflict is experienced, received, and judged.

Women are often expected to be accommodating. Men are often rewarded for dominance. Marginalized identities are policed for tone and 'appropriateness.' These double standards shape our emotional energy and limit authentic expression.

COACH'S INSIGHT

If you've been taught that your anger makes you 'difficult', your sadness makes you 'too sensitive', or your directness makes you 'aggressive'—this workbook is your permission slip to reclaim your voice.

Conflict isn't just interpersonal—it's systemic. Part of your healing may be refusing to play roles that shrink your truth.

RESEARCH SPOTLIGHT

Hochschild's work on 'emotional labor' reveals that women, especially in service or caregiving roles, are expected to manage others' emotions while suppressing their own—leading to increased emotional burnout and resentment (Hochschild, 1983; Nadal et al., 2014).

CASE STUDY

A Latina professional was labeled 'abrasive' in performance reviews. Through coaching, she reframed this narrative and used assertive scripts to increase her confidence, improve communication, and elevate her persuasiveness. Six months later, she was promoted—and still 100% herself.

A Black professional repeatedly silenced himself in team meetings to avoid being seen as 'difficult'. Through coaching, he reclaimed his voice and negotiated a role with more autonomy and cultural alignment.

Exercise 32:   Emotional Labor Log & Role Reversal Exercise (Section 6.6)

- Emotional Labor Log: Track one week of situations where you managed *others'* emotions. Reflect on whether this was by choice or expectation.

- Role Reversal Exercise: Imagine how the conflict would unfold if you swapped gender, racial, or identity roles with the other person. What changes?

- Journal Prompt: What would conflict look like if you were completely free from others' stereotypes or biases about you?

_____

_____

_____

_____

SECTION 7:
MASTERING CONFLICT IN HIGH-STAKES MOMENTS

'The harder the conflict, the more glorious the triumph.'
~ Thomas Paine

7.1 WHAT MAKES A MOMENT 'HIGH-STAKES'

High-stakes conflict is not about shouting — it's about the weight behind the words. These moments threaten something sacred: identity, trust, emotional safety, or the relationship's future. High-stakes conflict is defined less by the topic discussed or argued over, and more by the perceived threat – a threat to identity, belonging, status, safety, or the future. It's not always about the volume — it's about the emotional risk. A quiet conversation about betrayal can feel more threatening than a loud disagreement about dishes.

When the stakes feel high, people become hypervigilant. Every word is loaded. Every glance is interpreted. The nervous system takes over. This is when rational thought leaves and survival instincts take center stage.

What makes a conflict feel high-stakes can vary wildly: infidelity, money, a repeated betrayal, a professional reputation on the line, or even longstanding unresolved tension.

During these moments, the brain scans for threats. The stakes feel high because we believe the outcome will fundamentally alter the relationship or how we're perceived.

Learning to identify when you're entering a high-stakes moment is the first step in preventing reactivity and choosing conscious engagement.

COACH'S INSIGHT

In my coaching sessions with clients, I often ask, *'What feels at risk right now?'* High-stakes conflict triggers deeper fears — of being abandoned, misunderstood, controlled. Learning to name the perceived threat calms the nervous system and puts you back in the driver's seat.

Many of my clients don't recognize a moment as high-stakes until after the damage is done. If you notice increased tension, a surge of adrenaline, or a strong urge to shut down or lash out — it's likely you're already in the zone.

RESEARCH SPOTLIGHT

In a 2006 study published in *Emotion*, Eisenberger and colleagues found that perceived social rejection activates the same neural circuits as physical pain. This means conflict that threatens connection, or identity, can literally physically hurt — and trigger pain-avoidant behavior like defensiveness or withdrawal.

A 2021 meta-analysis in the *Journal of Family Psychology*, Kluwer and colleagues found that perceived power imbalances in romantic conflict were significantly correlated with heightened stress responses and poor outcomes. Simply put, when one or both people feel emotionally unsafe, the brain treats the conversation like a battle.

Exercise 33: Identify a High-Stakes Trigger (Section 7.1)

Think of a recurring high-stakes conflict or conversation that leaves you emotionally exhausted.

- What about this situation feels threatening (e.g., rejection, loss of control, shame)?

_____
_____
_____
_____

- How does your body react in the moment? Describe it in detail.

_____
_____
_____
_____

- What is the story your mind tells you when this happens?

_____
_____
_____
_____

- Now challenge that narrative: What's another possible interpretation?

_____
_____
_____
_____

7.2 WHY YOUR BRAIN HIJACKS YOU IN CONFLICT

During emotionally charged moments, the amygdala — your brain's alarm system — floods your body with stress hormones. Logic and empathy take a backseat. The amygdala is the part of your brain responsible for mobilizing fear, emotions, and motivation. Its name means 'almond' because it is almond-shaped.

If you see something that frightens you – a snake, a bear in the woods, a stranger following you at night -- your amygdala is the emotional center signaling your body when to panic. If the fear is warranted, then this signaling system is helpful. Yet, this panic response can be maladaptive if you're panicking and overreacting to situations that aren't warranted, such as public speaking, or fear of rejection on a date, etc.

In conflict, the amygdala's job is to protect — not to help you stay calm. Once activated, it hijacks the rational brain. Your body becomes flooded with cortisol and adrenaline. Your heart races, your muscles tighten, and your perception narrows.

You may speak without thinking, misread the other person's intentions, or jump to catastrophic conclusions. This is not a failure of willpower — it's biology. Knowing this lets you take it less personally and intervene more effectively.

This is known as an 'amygdala hijack,' a term coined by psychologist Daniel Goleman. Your thinking brain (prefrontal cortex) is temporarily offline. You respond from instinct, not intention.

That's why it's common to say things you later regret or feel unable to articulate what you truly mean. The goal isn't to avoid conflict — it's to restore enough calm to re-engage your higher brain.

COACH'S INSIGHT

When I see couples escalate rapidly, I remind them: the goal is not perfect calm, it's recovery. If you can shorten the time it takes to recognize the hijack and reset, you're building conflict resilience.

RESEARCH SPOTLIGHT

Neuroscientist Joseph LeDoux found that signals from the thalamus reach the amygdala before the cortex — meaning your emotional brain reacts before your rational brain processes the data. This explains why you often 'feel before you think' in conflict.

CASE STUDY

During a tense negotiation, Michelle felt dismissed by a colleague. Her heart raced, voice escalated, and she snapped. Later, she couldn't explain why it upset her so much. Upon reflection, she realized it reminded her of how her father used to interrupt her — triggering unresolved emotional memory, not just workplace frustration.

Exercise 34: Catching the Hijack (Section 7.2)

Recall a recent argument that escalated beyone where you wanted.

- When did your thinking go offline?

_____

_____

_____

_____

- What physical signs (tight jaw, racing thoughts, shallow breathing) did you notice?

_____

_____

- Write a sentence you wish you had said instead of what came out?

- What would help you self-regulate faster in that moment next time?

7.3 THE WINDOW OF TOLERANCE (AND WHY YOU LEAVE IT)

The 'Window of Tolerance' (Dan Siegel, MD) describes the emotional bandwidth in which you can think, feel, and respond with flexibility. Inside the window, you're balanced — aware of emotions but not overwhelmed by them. When you're inside your Window of Tolerance, you're able to stay grounded, curious, and flexible.

The more trauma or chronic stress you've experienced, the narrower your window tends to be. But it can widen with self-regulation skills, body awareness, and co-regulation with safe people.

Outside the window, you're in a trauma-adjacent state that manifests in core expressions:

- Emotional dysregulation: difficulty modulating emotional reactions
- Hyperarousal (fight or flight): You're angry, impulsive, and over-verbalizing.
- Hypoarousal (freeze or fawn): You're withdrawn, flat, unable to think clearly.

The narrower your window, the quicker you escalate or shut down. The good news? The window can be expanded with awareness and regulation.

COACH'S INSIGHT

I teach clients to use their bodies as a barometer. Shallow breath? Tense jaw? Cold fingers? You've probably exited the window. Naming it gives you a lever to pause, breathe, and return to presence.

Clients often say, *'It all happened so fast.'* That's your cue. If you can name what's happening — *'I'm leaving my window'* — you can pause and redirect before things spiral.

RESEARCH SPOTLIGHT

Dan Siegel's neurobiological model of the Window of Tolerance is now a staple in trauma therapy.

In 2020, Chamberlain and colleagues in *Frontiers in Psychology* confirmed its utility in identifying states of resilience vs. reactivity across clinical populations.

Exercise 35: Practice Tool - Map Your Window of Tolerance (Section 7.3)

- Describe how it feels when you're within your Window of Tolerance (thoughts, emotions, body cues).

_____

_____

_____

_____

- Now list your signs of hyperarousal (fight/flight) and hypoarousal (freeze/fawn).

_____

_____

_____

_____

- Identify 3 tools that bring you back into your window (e.g., deep breathing, walking, naming your state out loud).

1. _____
2. _____
3. _____

7.4 HOW TO RECOGNIZE FIGHT, FLIGHT, FREEZE, FAWN

These stress responses are not just survival tools — they shape how we argue, avoid, or over-accommodate in conflict. These are your nervous system's ancient responses to threat.

But they also shape your conflict habits:

- Fight:
    - What it looks like: Aggression, control, blaming, criticizing, arguing
    - The Outcome: You try to win or control the narrative.
- Flight:
    - What it looks like: Overworking, avoiding confrontation, physically leaving
    - The Outcome: You shut down the conversation or leave.
- Freeze:
    - What it looks like: Shutdown, dissociation, inability to speak or act
    - The Outcome: You go blank, unsure what to say.
- Fawn:
    - What it looks like: People-pleasing, appeasement, self-erasure to maintain peace
    - The Outcome: You appease the other to avoid tension.

Understanding your pattern helps you stop blaming yourself or others. It gives language to instinct — and from language comes awareness, understanding, and choice.

Each person has a dominant pattern, but context matters. The goal is to recognize your pattern and build awareness without shame.

COACH'S INSIGHT

We don't just inherit attachment styles — we inherit conflict survival styles. Knowing yours helps you make conscious shifts.

- Fighters can learn to ask instead of assert.
- Flighters can learn to sit with uncomfortable emotions and be more assertive.
- Freezers can learn to be intentional on how they want to resolve the conflict.

- Fawners can learn to pause before over-accommodating.

RESEARCH SPOTLIGHT

In 2022, in the *Journal of Psychological Trauma,* Nicolaides and Tull published findings showing that fawn responses — historically understudied — are linked to early attachment injury and are disproportionately present in high-conflict relationships with trauma histories.

CASE STUDY

When Jake and Tara argued, Jake often walked out (flight) while Tara begged him to stay and fix it immediately (fawn). Each saw the other's response as abandonment or control — when really, they were coping with stress in opposing ways. Learning this gave them compassion, and they agreed on a 'cool-off, then reconnect' plan.

Exercise 36: Know Your Stress Response Pattern (Section 7.4)

- Which response (fight, flight, freeze, fawn) do you default to?

_____
_____
_____
_____

- Describe what that looks like in your body, behavior, and thoughts.

_____
_____
_____
_____

- Identify a recent moment where this response showed up.

_____
_____
_____
_____

- Write out a more intentional response you'd like to try next time.

_____
_____
_____
_____

SECTION 8:
REPAIRING AFTER RUPTURE

'What we don't need in the midst of struggle is shame for being human.'
~ Brené Brown

8.1 WHY REPAIR IS MORE IMPORTANT THAN 'NEVER FIGHTING'

I opened this workbook in Section 1 with a very poignant quote from Simon Sinek, which warrants repeating here:

'What makes great relationships great is not that you get along all the time. The best marriages, the best relationships, they aren't free of conflict – it's that they know how to resolve conflict peacefully.'
~ Simon Sinek

Conflict is inevitable. What determines relationship strength isn't how well we avoid conflict — it's how skillfully we repair after it.

Many people believe that the absence of conflict defines successful relationships. But true connection isn't forged in harmony — it's tempered in the aftermath of disruption. Repair is the gold standard of resilience.

When we engage in rupture-repair cycles with awareness, each cycle becomes an opportunity to grow deeper trust. The process of circling back, owning your part, and tending to emotional injury models maturity and emotional accountability. It's not about keeping the peace — it's about restoring it consciously.

Research from the Gottman Institute shows that the strongest relationships are not conflict-free. In fact, repair attempts — even imperfect ones — are a better predictor of long-term relationship health than the frequency of arguments.

Repair gives the nervous system closure. Without it, relationships stay activated — even when things seem 'fine.' The body remembers unresolved tension. Repair calms the body, rebuilds trust, and keeps the emotional bridge intact.

When people believe fighting equals failure, they suppress problems until they explode. This false ideal blocks vulnerability, learning, and deeper connection.

COACH'S INSIGHT

I've coached executives and couples alike who believed that emotional distance meant maturity. But emotional safety isn't created by silence — it's built by rupture and repair. The courage to revisit hard conversations is often the turning point in deep relationships.

Couples I work with often assume that not arguing means they're doing well. But emotional distance often masquerades as peace. I've seen more damage done by quiet avoidance than loud arguing. Healthy relationships don't avoid rupture — they get good at repair.

RESEARCH SPOTLIGHT

John and Julie Gottman (2015) found that in stable relationships, partners respond to repair attempts — even clumsy ones — 86% of the time. In distressed relationships, that number drops below 30%. It's not about perfect words; it's about willingness to reconnect.

In a 2019 study from the *Journal of Social and Personal Relationships*, Williamson and colleagues found that couples who made consistent repair attempts post-conflict reported greater emotional intimacy, improved conflict confidence, and lower rates of emotional withdrawal.

Exercise 37:   Personal Affirmation for Repair (Section 8.1)

- Think of a time when a relationship grew stronger after a conflict. What made that possible?
- When have you avoided conflict in an effort to keep the peace? What did that cost you?

    Exercise:
    Create a personal affirmation for how you will approach conflict and repair moving forward.

    Example: 'I don't avoid conflict — I repair through it with strength and care.'

_____

_____

_____

8.2 THE ANATOMY OF A RUPTURE

A rupture is any moment where trust is strained, emotional safety is broken, or connection is interrupted. A rupture is a breach in connection. It doesn't always feel catastrophic.

Sometimes it's subtle: eye rolls, avoidance, broken agreements, forgetting something important, dismissing a concern, or prioritizing work over presence. Some ruptures are loud — shouting, betrayal, name-calling.

But the emotional residue builds. Without acknowledgment, these micro-injuries layer into macro damage. Unacknowledged ruptures build emotional scar tissue. Over time, that calcifies into resentment, distance, and even contempt.

Ruptures come in three main forms:

1. **Emotional injury** – Feeling dismissed, invalidated, or unseen.
2. **Behavioral breach** – An action (or inaction) that breaks an explicit or implicit agreement.
3. **Energetic withdrawal** – Pulling away without naming it, creating emotional absence.

The sooner you can recognize the rupture, the easier it is to repair without compounding it.

Healthy conflict management requires learning to name the rupture, take responsibility, and initiate repair before resentment hardens.

COACH'S INSIGHT

The longer a rupture goes unacknowledged, the more meaning we attach to it. Your mind starts writing stories to make sense of the gap. Most of them are inaccurate. Repair prevents story-building by filling in the emotional blank.

RESEARCH SPOTLIGHT

Sue Johnson (2008), founder of Emotionally Focused Therapy (EFT), found that unresolved attachment ruptures — even minor ones — lead to long-term insecurity if not addressed, reinforcing cycles of withdrawal or protest behavior.

CASE STUDY

Luis, a team leader, frequently cut off his colleague Rachel in meetings. Rachel eventually stopped speaking up. When HR flagged the dynamic, Luis initially denied wrongdoing. But when he learned about rupture patterns, he realized his behavior echoed his father's dismissiveness — and initiated a private apology and a structural change in meeting formats. That one repair re-engaged Rachel and shifted the team culture.

Elena noticed her partner, Chris, had grown distant after a disagreement about parenting. When she finally asked, he admitted he felt unheard and shamed. That moment of emotional honesty led to a powerful repair. They agreed to check in weekly to avoid small grievances piling into bigger ones. Identifying rupture early prevented further emotional erosion.

Exercise 38: Anatomy of a Rupture - Journal Prompt (Section 8.2)

- Identify a recent moment that felt like a rupture (personal or professional).
- What was the behavior, and what was the deeper impact?

    Exercise: Complete the following statements:

    - 'The behavior I noticed was _____'
    - 'It left me feeling _____'
    - 'What I needed in that moment was _____'

8.3 COMMON MYTHS THAT PREVENT REPAIR

Repair requires vulnerability — and vulnerability can feel risky. That's why myths about repair persist; they provide convenient barriers to us stepping into that vulnerability. Yet the cost we pay by not stepping into that vulnerability is disconnection and limited capacity to repair

Myth 1: *'If I didn't intend to hurt you, I shouldn't need to apologize.'*

Truth: Intent doesn't erase impact. You can hurt someone unintentionally and still be responsible for your part.

Myth 2: *'They're being too sensitive — they need to get over it.'*

Truth: Sensitivity isn't weakness. Admitting to pain and difficult emotions is actually courageous, and it deepens understanding and improves connection. Dismissing emotions deepens the rupture.

Myth 3: *'Apologizing is giving up my power.'*

Truth: Apologizing from a grounded place is a profound act of strength.

Myth 4: *'Apologizing makes me weak.'*

Truth: Repair is not submission — it's strength under control. Taking ownership builds credibility.

Myth 5: *'They should come to me first.'*

Truth: Waiting for the other person to blink first creates a power struggle, not a path forward.

These myths protect the ego, but sabotage connection.

COACH'S INSIGHT

Repair doesn't mean taking blame for everything. It means saying: *'I value this connection more than my ego in this moment.'* I often ask clients: *'Do you want to be right — or do you want to be effective, do you want to restore?'*

When clients say, *'I don't want to reward their behavior by apologizing,'* I remind them: repair is not about reward. It's about re-aligning your values with your communication. You can set boundaries and still say, *'I didn't handle that well.'*

RESEARCH SPOTLIGHT

A 2022 meta-review in *Clinical Psychology Review* conducted by Donovan and Furlong found that perceived sincerity in repair attempts — even more than content of the apology — was the strongest predictor of forgiveness and reconnection.

Exercise 39: Unpacking Your Repair Myths (Section 8.3)

- Which myth around repair do you most struggle with (e.g., *'apologizing makes me weak'*)?
- Where did that belief come from? What would it take to challenge it?

Exercise:

Write a short internal script challenging your most limiting belief about repair.

Replace it with a healthier alternative.

_____

_____

8.4. HOW TO INITIATE REPAIR WITHOUT LOSING POWER

Repair doesn't require groveling. It requires courage, clarity, and grounded language. Repair begins with regulation. If you're still flooded with emotion, your words will land defensively. Step back, breathe, then re-engage from intention.

Use the 3 Rs of Repair:

- *Recognize* the rupture: Acknowledge the rupture without over-explaining. When we over-explain, we seem defensive.
  - *'That didn't go how I wanted.'*
  - *'I know things felt off after our last talk.'*

- *Responsibility* (without over-owning): Own the impact of the rupture and its fallout, not just what your intentions were.
  - *'I interrupted you, and that made things worse.'*
  - *'I realize I came off as defensive, and that probably shut you down.'*

- *Re-engage* with consent: Invite and offer re-connection, without being demanding.
  - *'I'd like to revisit that. Are you open to a fresh conversation?'*
  - *'Can we take another shot at this when you're ready?'*

Repair isn't about perfection. It's about presence, ownership, and honoring the relationship over the argument.

Power is not lost in repair — it's earned in the willingness to lead with emotional integrity.

CASE STUDY

David, an executive, unintentionally shamed a direct report in a meeting. The next morning, instead of brushing it off, he pulled her aside and said, *'I spoke too sharply. That wasn't fair. I appreciate your work and your voice in the room.'* That 20-second moment restored morale and earned long-term respect.

Samantha, a VP at a healthcare firm, accidentally forwarded a private conversation about a colleague's performance. She apologized immediately, explained the mistake without defensiveness, and then gave the colleague space while remaining available to discuss and process it. Weeks later, the colleague thanked her — not for the apology, but for not disappearing after it. That is leaning in and showing leadership through repair.

COACH'S INSIGHT

If you're afraid that repairing makes you weak, flip the question:

'Who do you trust more — someone who denies harm, or someone who owns it with dignity?' Real leaders — in life and work — know how to do hard things gently.

RESEARCH SPOTLIGHT

In workplace studies by the *Harvard Business Review*, Edmondson found teams that regularly practiced post-conflict repair had 35% higher psychological safety and retention rates. Repair boosts team health — not just interpersonal rapport.

Exercise 40: Interpersonal Repair Script Practice (Section 8.4)

Reflection Prompt:
- What fears come up when you consider initiating a repair conversation?
- How would it feel to prioritize emotional integrity over being right?

Script Practice:
Choose one of the following templates and write out a full repair script you could use:

- *'I know our last interaction didn't land well. I want to revisit it with more care.'*
- *'I recognize I hurt you with my words. That wasn't my intention, but I take full responsibility.'*
- *'Can we have a do-over on that moment? It matters to me that we get back in sync.'*

_____
_____
_____
_____
_____
_____

SECTION 9:
PREVENTING CONFLICT BEFORE IT STARTS

'Let go or be dragged.'
~ old Zen proverb

9.1 THE HIDDEN TRIGGERS THAT SPARK CONFLICT EARLY

Many of the biggest conflicts begin not with a fight, but with a flicker — a raised eyebrow, a dismissive sigh, or a slightly delayed response. These are 'micro-triggers,' small cues that tap into deeper, often unconscious emotional material, and they often go unnoticed until they've stacked into full-blown resentment.

Micro-triggers stem from past emotional wounds, attachment patterns, and unspoken insecurities. What feels like an overreaction in the moment is often a reaction to dozens of past moments stored in the nervous system.

Micro-triggers are often expressed through:

- Tone of voice
- Word choice
- Cadence of phrasing
- Perceived disinterest or withdrawal

The first step in conflict prevention is self-awareness: Can I identify what reliably activates me? Can I name the hidden stories I attach to those activations? The earlier you catch a trigger, the more options you have to regulate it.

When we're unaware of these triggers, they accumulate. Conflict becomes inevitable, not because of the issue itself, but because of what it activates under the surface.

Learning to name and normalize early triggers helps you pause before escalation.

COACH'S INSIGHT

I once worked with a CFO who frequently found himself in defensive arguments with his COO. It wasn't about performance — it was tone. The COO had a habit of maintaining a flat affect, which the CFO interpreted as a lack of judgment. Once the CFO learned to name the story he was telling himself (*'He thinks I'm incompetent'*), it diffused the negative charge of their interaction. He could then choose response over reaction.

I often ask clients to map their 'conflict pre-game': what happens in the 10 minutes before a blow-up? Most realize it's a buildup of subtle signs they ignored. Prevention starts with awareness.

RESEARCH SPOTLIGHT

In a 2022 meta-analysis by Kashdan and colleagues, published in *Emotion Review*, researchers found that early detection of emotional triggers reduced the likelihood of escalation by up to 48%. The key was not the size of the trigger, but the speed of recognition and regulation.

A 2020 study in the *Journal of Conflict Resolution*, Remland and colleagues found that over 65% of workplace disputes traced back to perceived tone or body language—not the content of the message itself.

CASE STUDY

A couple, Dana and Marcus, constantly fought over what seemed like small things: texts left unread, dishes in the sink, laundry left in the dryer. When we explored their patterns, it became clear these actions triggered old beliefs — Dana felt unimportant, Marcus felt micromanaged. Once they learned to name these underlying feelings, they created a 'check-in code word' to pause and reset before conflict erupted.

Exercise 41: Create Your Trigger Map (Section 9.1)

Reflection Prompt:

- What types of behaviors, tones, or situations tend to trigger you most easily?
- What old stories or experiences might be linked to these triggers?

Exercise:

Create your personal 'Trigger Map.'

Write down:

- Common triggers – what triggers lead to conflict, defensive reaction, or emotional activation for you?

_____
_____
_____
_____

- Associated emotions – what emotions arise when you are triggered?

_____
_____
_____
_____

- A new intentional response you want to try – what new response are you committing to try rather than your prior (less adaptive) pattern of responding?

    (Example: Trigger = being interrupted ⊠ Emotion = disrespected ⊠ New Response = pause, breathe, name it calmly)

_____
_____
_____
_____

9.2 WHAT PSYCHOLOGICAL SAFETY LOOKS LIKE IN ACTION

Psychological safety is the invisible foundation of healthy conflict. It's the trust that even when emotions rise, the relationship won't rupture. It's the felt sense that you can speak up, disagree, express emotion, or ask questions without fear of punishment or rejection. When we feel psychologically safe, we feel we can be our authentic selves in the presence of others.

In practice, this looks like:

- Being able to say, 'I disagree' without fear of retribution
- Naming your feelings without being gaslit
- Apologizing without having your mistake thrown back at you later

In relationships, psychological safety means:

- You feel heard even when the other person disagrees.
- Mistakes are met with curiosity, not criticism.
- You trust that honesty won't be weaponized later.

We humans like predictability; it helps us feel contained, comfortable, and safe. Thus, creating safety starts with consistency. People need to know how you show up when things go sideways — not just when they're calm.

This safety isn't accidental. It's intentionally built through consistency, emotional regulation, and attuned communication.

COACH'S INSIGHT

The safest relationships are not the quietest — they're the ones where both people can bring their full selves to the interaction. I ask clients: *'Does your relationship welcome the truth, or only the agreeable version of it?'* If it only welcomes agreeableness and does not allow truth and honesty a place at the table, that is a disconnect that needs attention or it will eventually lead to breakdown.

A client once said, *'I only feel safe when we're not arguing.'* I challenged her: real safety means feeling secure *even when* you're disagreeing. That's when trust is tested. That's when repair matters most.

RESEARCH SPOTLIGHT

Amy Edmondson's foundational research at the Harvard Business School on psychological safety showed that teams with high safety have better performance and fewer errors. Psychological safety is the single best predictor of high-functioning teams. In relationships, it predicts openness, emotional resilience and sustained intimacy over time (Edmondson, 2018).

CASE STUDY

Jared and Lily had repeated conflicts over parenting. When they started using a weekly 'neutral zone space' to talk about emotionally charged topics without interruptions or judgment, they fought less. The safety of the space reduced anxiety and increased curiosity — allowing them to problem-solve without spiraling.

Exercise 42: Your Safety Contract (Section 9.2)

Reflection Prompt:

- In what relationships do you feel the most emotionally safe? Why?
- In which relationships do you feel you have to hold back or self-censor? Why?

Exercise:

Write a 'safety contract' for a key relationship.

Include:

- What helps you feel safe: _____
- What undermines your safety: _____
- One step you'll take to increase safety this week:

_____

_____

_____

_____

9.3 PROACTIVE COMMUNICATION HABITS THAT PREVENT BLOWUPS

When it comes to navigating communication problems, the best defense is having a good offense. Most people wait until conflict has already emerged prior to initiating communication. Prevention means building communication habits that catch disconnection early. The best conflict prevention strategy is good communication hygiene. This means setting up regular rhythms of clear, connective dialogue — not just reacting in crisis moments.

These include:

- Checking in before tension builds -- *'Anything feel off between us this week?'*

- Naming emotions instead of projecting them – *'I'm feeling edgy today — not about you, just overwhelmed.'*

- Using buffers like shared rituals (walks, debriefs, end-of-day reflections) to maintain connection. You can also use pre-agreed-upon code words to highlight a pain point. Instead of saying, *'You left the dishes in the sink again!'*, you code this and just say 'Code 28' (or whatever code word you agree on.). By connecting the feedback to a neutral word or number, you deflate the negative emotional association to the prior history of 'complaining' about that issue.

- Level setting stress levels to foster understanding and support -- *'On a scale of 1-100, I'm only at about 40% today for my stress capacity.'*

Conflict prevention is a lifestyle — not a last resort.

Examples include:

- Weekly check-ins (with partners or teams)

- Using clarifying statements instead of assumptions: *'Can I check if I understood you correctly?'*

- Naming your emotional state before it spills over: *'I'm feeling tense — can we slow this down?'*

When people feel heard and understood early, they don't have to shout to be noticed later.

COACH'S INSIGHT

Most blowups are failed prevention. Think of communication like brushing your teeth — you don't do it because things are bad or only when you have a cavity, you do it so they don't get bad. Build in small, consistent habits to connect with those in your life – at home, at work, in the community.

I coach leaders to hold 'temperature check' conversations weekly — short, structured, and intentional. These prevent misinterpretations from festering into full-blown friction. In relationships, the same principle applies: if you keep the air clear, there's less static later.

RESEARCH SPOTLIGHT

Gordon and colleagues, in a 2021 study in the *Journal of Social and Personal Relationships*, found that couples who scheduled 15-minute weekly check-ins experienced a 31% reduction in relational tension, increased emotional attunement and higher relationship satisfaction scores over time.

CASE STUDY

Tasha and Brian implemented a Sunday evening check-in over tea. Initially awkward, it became their most connected time of the week. They noticed they were arguing less — not because tension disappeared, but because it got addressed earlier.

Exercise 43: The Board Meeting (Section 9.3)

I recommend to my coaching clients to have a weekly 'Board Meeting', as a way to emotionally connect and align on goals and priorities. This is one of the techniques recommended by Jordan Peterson, among others.

Frequency & Duration: At least 60 minutes per week in open, intentional conversation.

Discussion areas:

1. Personal updates – what you accomplished
2. Practical/logistical household matters – what needs to be handled in the coming week
3. Needs, Wants, and Non-negotiables
4. Shared goals, vision and plans – for the upcoming week and month

Benefits:

- Builds intimacy through active listening
- Keeps logistical issues from overwhelming downtime
- Strengthens shared understanding and alignment on future priorities

Why This Format Works

- Structure prevents drift: By designating a set time weekly, important topics don't get lost in unscheduled, ad-hoc exchanges or shutdowns at dinner.

- Instead of emotional "drive-by" moments, both partners can prepare and enter the conversation with attention and intention.
- Shared problem-solving: The meeting becomes a cooperative forum, not a battleground or emotional dump—better for conflict, planning, and intimacy alike

Sample Format for the 60-Minute Weekly Meeting

Time	Focus
5–10 min	Start warmly—share something positive or express gratitude to set a supportive tone.
10–20 min	Personal updates—how each person is doing, emotionally and practically (work, stress, etc.).
20 min	Household logistics —upcoming events, responsibilities, finances, chores, childcare, etc.
5–10 min	Future-alignment—shared vision and expectations for the week; reassure, reaffirm unity.

Exercise 44: Your Escalation Prevention Ritual (Section 9.3)

Reflection Prompt:

- Think of a recent conflict. What could have been said earlier to prevent it?
- With Whom can you implement a consistent check-in habit (partner, friend, team)?

Exercise:

Design your personal 'Prevention Ritual.'

- Choose a day/time and method (verbal, written, shared walk, etc.).
- Commit to a weekly check-in and list 3 questions you'll use (e.g., 'Is there anything we've been avoiding?' 'How are we doing this week?', etc.).

Q1. _____

Q2. _____

Q3. _____

9.4 HOW TO BUILD TRUST WITHOUT OVER-EXPLAINING YOURSELF

Many high-achievers over-explain to preempt conflict or avoid criticism. But over-explaining often signals insecurity, not strength. It erodes trust because it can sound like justification rather than honesty, and is often perceived as guilt, excuse-making, or defensiveness — especially in emotionally charged moments.

You don't have to justify every 'no,' explain every boundary, or rationalize every decision.

'Clear, confident communication creates safety. Rambling undermines it.'

The goal is to speak with calm authority:

- *'Here's my decision.'*
- *'That doesn't work for me.'*
- *'I'm open to feedback, but I've made my choice.'*

Confidence without arrogance, paired with accountability, creates calm authority in relationships.

You build trust by:

- Speaking directly and succinctly
- Letting silence do some of the work
- Being consistent in actions, not just words

Trust grows not just from what you say — but from how clearly and calmly you say it.

COACH'S INSIGHT

I worked with a physician who felt guilty every time he said no – to his wife, his kids, his staff. As a result of the guilt, he tended to over-explain and came across as defensive and insecure in his decisions. We practiced one-sentence boundaries – making clear statements of his stance on a given issue or decision – followed by a pause. He was shocked at how many people appreciated the brief explanation, and how very few of them wanted 'more' explanation. Most just wanted clarity.

You don't need a 10-minute backstory to justify your 'no' or your boundary. I teach my coaching clients to replace explanations with clarity: *'Here's what I can offer.'* Full stop. Trust often grows in the space after the sentence.

RESEARCH SPOTLIGHT

Drawing on research from the *Harvard Negotiation Project (2019)*, Stone and colleagues found that concise, boundary-based communication was rated more trustworthy and emotionally intelligent than elaborative justifications in both professional and personal settings. This effect was even stronger in emotionally charged conversations.

CASE STUDY

In navigating relationship conflict with his fiancée, Andrew realized he always over-explained because he feared being misunderstood. Once he began stating his needs clearly and directly, his partner felt more heard, understood and respected — and less overwhelmed. Their arguments dropped significantly.

Exercise 45:   One-Line Boundaries (Section 9.4)

Reflection Prompt:

- When do you tend to over-explain? What are you afraid might happen if you don't explain a lot?

- What would it feel like to state your truth calmly and stop there?

Exercise:

Practice the 'One-Line Boundary: exercise:

- Write 3 examples of clear, concise boundaries or decisions, like:

    - *'I'm not available this weekend.' OR 'That doesn't work for me.' OR 'I need a day to think before I respond.'*

1. _____
2. _____
3. _____

Say each one out loud, pause, and sit with any discomfort without adding more explanation.

SECTION 10:
NAVIGATING CONFLICT DURING SEPARATION AND DIVORCE

'What you're not changing, you're choosing.'
~ Anonymous

'Divorce is like a gunfight where everyone is rooting for the bullets.'
~ James Sexton

10.1 WHY CONFLICT DURING DIVORCE FEELS SO PERSONAL (EVEN WHEN IT'S NOT)

Divorce is rarely just about logistics. It exposes core wounds—fear of abandonment, betrayal, failure, rejection, inadequacy. That's why even small disagreements can feel massive. Even practical disagreements often carry emotional weight that predates the current conflict.

If your divorce involved legal action, the legal process may ask you to 'stay neutral' but your nervous system interprets everything as personal. A slow reply can feel like rejection. A request for more custody time can feel like erasure. A request to alter a visitation schedule may feel like a challenge to your value as a parent. A financial dispute may feel like confirmation that you're unworthy of respect.

These interpretations are emotional, not logical. But they shape how we respond. Recognizing this dynamic allows you to separate the person from the pattern — allowing you to regulate the response rather than react to the emotion.

Understanding that your body is reacting to perceived threat—not just the current situation—helps you regulate before reacting. When you separate meaning from story, you reclaim your peace.

COACH'S INSIGHT

A client once shared with me, *'It's like I'm constantly waiting to be attacked, even in emails.'* We discovered that her ex's passive tone mirrored her father's critical detachment. She wasn't fighting her ex—she was reliving an old pattern, and as such, fighting the ghost of her father. That insight shifted her entire approach.

I remind clients that pain during divorce doesn't mean you're doing it wrong — it means you're human. But letting pain run the conversation ensures more damage. The more you can depersonalize, the more you reclaim your power.

RESEARCH SPOTLIGHT

The *American Psychological Association* (APA, 2019) reports that unresolved emotional injuries—not legal disputes—are the main cause of prolonged high-conflict divorce. These are often fueled less by the issues themselves and more by unresolved attachment injuries and poor emotional regulation (APA, 2019).

CASE STUDY

Laura and Ben were battling over finances. In mediation, the issue wasn't money—it was that Ben felt shut out of major decisions. Once Laura acknowledged that fear, the financial plan became easier to negotiate. Naming the emotional truth unblocked the logistical solution.

Exercise 46: The Conflict Letter (Section 10.1)

Reflection Prompt:

- What makes certain statements or behaviors feel like a personal attack?
- Can you identify the deeper emotional wound that gets triggered in those moments?

Exercise:

Write a letter (not to be sent) to your ex explaining how a recent conflict made you feel, and what old story it activated. Then write a new narrative that affirms your worth and boundaries regardless of their behavior. Do not send the letter! The letter is for you, your reflection and your growth – not for them.

10.2 THE PUSH-PULL OF ATTACHMENT AND AUTONOMY IN SEPARATION

One of the most confusing dynamics in separation is wanting closeness and distance at the same time. This ambivalence plays out in mixed signals, lingering resentment, or unconscious sabotage of the separation process.

Separation activates a psychological paradox: we crave both connection and distance.

You may feel hurt by the other person's behavior, but still check their social media. You may initiate boundaries, but secretly hope they'll break through them to prove they care.

You might find yourself:

- Wanting reassurance while resenting the other person
- Feeling relief and grief in the same breath
- Needing space but also fearing abandonment

This push-pull is normal. This ambivalence is common. What matters is becoming aware of it — so it doesn't lead to emotional whiplash or inconsistent boundaries. But when unacknowledged, it leads to hot-and-cold behavior that prolongs suffering and confuses everyone involved. The goal is to name your mixed emotions without acting from them impulsively.

COACH'S INSIGHT

I worked with a client who blocked and unblocked her ex on social media weekly. She called it 'boundary setting'—but it was really boundary testing. She wanted to prompt a response. When we identified her deeper longing for closure, she created space for healing instead of control.

Ambivalence is not weakness — it's grief in motion. You're losing a version of your life, not just a relationship. Honor the confusion. But don't use it as a reason to stay in reactive patterns.

RESEARCH SPOTLIGHT

Attachment theory shows that separations trigger deep-rooted safety mechanisms. Anxious types may seek connection; avoidant types may emotionally detach. Both can lead to escalated conflict if unmanaged. Research by Mikulincer & Shaver (2016) found that during separation, individuals with insecure attachment styles report higher emotional volatility, more ruminative thought, and lower co-parenting success rates.

CASE STUDY

David left a toxic marriage but couldn't stop emailing long reflections to his ex. He said his intention was 'to find peace.' In truth, he feared being forgotten. Through coaching, he learned to meet his emotional needs internally, get clarity on his wants and needs, and not by seeking re-entry into a dysfunctional dynamic.

Exercise 47: Mapping Attachment vs. Autonomy in Separation (Section 10.2)

Reflection Prompt:

- When do you feel most pulled toward your ex? Most repelled?
- What unmet need is behind each pull or push?

    Exercise:

    Draw two columns labeled ATTACHMENT and AUTONOMY. Under each, list:

    - Thoughts that arise
    - Emotions that surface
    - Unmet needs

Reflect on how you can honor both needs without acting reactively.

	Attachment	**Autonomy**
Thoughts that arise		
Emotions that surface		
Unmet Needs		

10.3 COMMON COMMUNICATION TRAPS AND HOW TO AVOID THEM

Communication is often the battlefield during separation. The way you communicate can either lead to a calm resolution or light a match in a tinderbox.

The most common traps include:

- Defending instead of clarifying
- Defensive texting: Explaining everything to justify yourself

- Digging into the past instead of solving the present issues
- Historical rehashing: Arguing about the past to gain an upper hand
- Reacting from hurt instead of responding with intention to repair
- Tone-policing: Getting stuck on delivery rather than a goal towards mutual understanding
- Ambiguous agreements: 'We'll figure it out later' becomes fuel for future fights

The key to effective and amicable communication is structure.

- ***Stay in the Present*** – Avoid rehashing old conflicts and instead remain focused on the current issue(s) to be resolved at the moment. In a literal sense, 'Pick your battles wisely.'

- ***Short Statements*** – Use bullet points rather than lengthy monologues. This promotes better attention from the other person and increases the likelihood of understanding.

- ***Time Limits*** – The energy behind animated conflict can continue for a long time, but productive discussion or even arguing has a half-life. As the argument continues, people become exhausted, resulting in a decrease in patience and understanding.

- ***Neutral Tone and Language*** –Based on the science of neuro-linguistic processing (NLP), good communication is not primarily based on the words we say. In fact, effective communication is impacted by 60% of our non-verbal communication, 30% tone, and only 10% by the words we choose.

- ***Take a Pause*** – One easy technique is to respond after reflection, not in the heat of a trigger. Take a breath, and take a pause. Ask yourself internally: *'Would I say this, or say it in this way, in front of my friends, or in a court proceeding, or at work?'* If you answer 'no', then take the time and rethink or rewrite your response.

- ***Pivot to Writin*** – If the atmosphere is too heated, consider moving away from a verbal dialogue (that is repeatedly and quickly devolving into yelling), and instead write out your perspectives to one another. This allows timing, cadence, and distance to process what the other person is sharing. It turns down the heat on the interaction.

COACH'S INSIGHT

I've seen co-parents avoid a year of court battles with one shift: learning to text like a lawyer and listen like a mediator. Clean language, clear agreements, emotional neutrality — that's the formula. If you don't give the other person fuel to ignite the fire, it tends to burn out.

All too often, we enter an argument with an unspoken or outspoken intent to 'win'. Yet arguments and conflicts are not to be won; they are things to unpack and unravel. The goal is not a zero-sum winner-takes-all approach. Rather the goal is to seek understanding and gain clarity towards a reasonable resolution.

A client once told me, *'I don't text emotionally—I just say what I feel.'* We pulled up his text messages and reviewed them. Every single message was a novel laced with blame. This needed correction. He now uses a 3-part rule: short, neutral, and forward-focused. His ex responded differently within a week.

RESEARCH SPOTLIGHT

According to the AFCC (*Association of Family and Conciliation Courts*, 2020), communication style during separation is the strongest predictor of whether parents will enter high-conflict litigation within 12 months. Emotionally neutral, consistent, and documented communication is the top predictor of decreased court involvement in co-parenting disputes.

CASE STUDY

Jamie and Chris had difficulties co-parenting. They used to argue over every school schedule change. Their problems were not a lack of intention or desire to cooperate; it was a lack of organization and structure. They implemented a shared Google Calendar and began using a family messaging app that restricted emotional content (i.e., Our Family Wizard (https://www.ourfamilywizard.com) ; Talking Parents (https://talkingparents.com). Fights dropped by 80%. The system handled what their tempers could not.

Exercise 48: Your Communication Reboot (Section 10.3)

Reflection Prompt:

- What's your default communication trap (defensiveness, rehashing, sarcasm)?
- What does it protect you from feeling?

    Exercise:

    Find a recent text or email thread. Rewrite your responses using:

    - Neutral tone
    - Present-focused language

- One clear request

Compare how each version might land emotionally with the reader.

10.4 NAVIGATING CO-PARENTING WITH BOUNDARIES, NOT BITTERNESS

You don't have to like your co-parent, but you do have to work with them if you share children. Co-parenting is not about being friends. It's about creating functional, child-focused systems even if the emotional relationship is broken.

Boundaries are the container that allows this system to work.

Boundaries are clear, internal guidelines you set for how YOU will engage with others and how you expect to be treated. They are based on your values, needs, emotional safety, and capacity, and they help define what's okay and what's not okay for you in relationships.

What Boundaries are NOT. These are controlling behaviors, ultimatums, or passive-aggressive attempts to change OTHERS, often mislabeled as boundaries. They attempt to manage someone else's behavior, rather than take responsibility for your own.

Setting clear boundaries includes:

- Having a neutral (think 'businesslike') tone in communication
- Establishing a clear division of responsibilities
- Respecting the other parent's time, space, and parenting style (even if you disagree, and to the extent it is not causing potential harm)

Boundaries are what protect your time, values, and emotional energy. They sound like:

BOUNDARY	NOT BOUNDARY
• 'I'm not available to respond to messages after 7 PM.' • 'I need 24 hours to make schedule changes.' • 'I'm not comfortable with yelling. I'll step away if that continues.' • 'I'm going to stick to the parenting plan we agreed to.'	• 'You can't call me after 7pm' • 'You can't expect me to drop everything and change in a day's notice.' • 'You have to stop yelling at me!' • 'You aren't following (or you need to follow) the parenting plan.'

Without clear boundaries, communication breaks down and bitterness and resentment can grow. Bitterness, however, infects the space between you — and kids absorb it. It shows up in tone, language, and small sabotage. Don't teach your kids that love equals blame. Show them it can coexist with boundaries and that it can exist within an amicable relationship. Bitterness may feel justified, but it often turns the child into a messenger or battleground. Boundaries protect you and the children as well as your peace.

COACH'S INSIGHT

One client kept telling her son, *'I'm sorry your dad didn't show up — he just doesn't care.'* She thought she was being honest. In reality, she was enlisting her child as an ally and sabotaging the child's relationship with his father. Once we identified this pattern, we began to reframe her approach. We practiced language like: *'I know you are disappointed. I will talk to your father, and I'm here now.'* The child felt more secure.

You're not just raising kids — you're modeling how to navigate tension. And yes, like it or not, you're modeling how to navigate a relationship – even if the relationship is no longer an intimate one, you still have a relationship as long as you are co-parents. When my coaching clients are working through this process, I ask them: *'Would you want your child to repeat the dynamic you're in right now? If not, change how you show up.'*

We've all heard 'Happy Wife, happy Life', but when it comes to co-parenting, the mantra is 'Keep communication alive, and the kids will thrive.'

RESEARCH SPOTLIGHT

A longitudinal study (Kelly & Emery, 2003) found that children in structured, low-conflict co-parenting arrangements showed similar well-being to those in intact families, while high-conflict co-parenting produced worse outcomes than divorce itself. Children in high-conflict co-parenting arrangements show higher rates of anxiety, depression, and academic disruption. What matters most is not whether parents are together, but how they treat each other after separation.

Whether you divorce or not is not the key impact on your children; it is HOW you divorce!

CASE STUDY

Erica and Joe co-parent two teens. After months of sarcasm and missed handoffs, they agreed to treat exchanges like business meetings. They limited verbal conversation and used a shared log for school updates, as well as a shared co-parenting app to handle communications in a controlled way. Within three months, their kids reported less anxiety and more stability.

Exercise 49: The Co-Parenting Values Card (Section 10.4)

Reflection Prompt:

- What boundary feels hardest to uphold with your co-parent?
- What fear or belief makes it difficult?

Exercise:

Create a 'Co-Parenting Values Card.' On one side, list values you want to model (e.g., respect, calm, consistency). On the other, list 3 boundary statements that align with those values. Keep this card as a daily guide.

Example:

Co-Parenting Values Card	
Values I want to Model	**Boundary Statements**
Respect	1 _____
Calm	_____
Emotional regulation	_____
Consistency	
	2 _____
_____	_____
_____	_____
	3 _____
_____	_____
_____	_____

SECTION 11:

HIGH-CONFLICT PERSONALITIES AND HOW TO MANAGE THEM

'Everything I've ever let go of has claw marks in it.'
~ David Foster Wallace

11.1. WHAT IS A HIGH-CONFLICT PERSONALITY? (AND WHAT IT'S NOT)

High-conflict personalities (HCPs) are not simply difficult or disagreeable people. They are individuals with chronic maladaptive patterns who consistently escalate conflict rather than resolve it, often relying on blame, distortion, and threats. HCPs can exist in personal, professional, or legal relationships. They tend to externalize responsibility and provoke extreme emotional reactions in others.

Importantly, HCP is not a diagnosis — it is a descriptive framework, it's a pattern of behavior. While individuals with clinical personality disorders may engage in high-conflict behavior, not all HCPs meet diagnostic thresholds.

HCPs show predictable behaviors such as splitting others into 'good' and 'bad', escalating minor issues into major problems, and responding poorly (i.e., defensively) to feedback or boundaries. Common features include an intense preoccupation with blame, emotional dysregulation, and difficulty accepting responsibility.

HCPs are what we call in the threat of violence mitigation field 'grievance collectors'; they never let a complaint or grievance go that they could not double down on and try to use to their advantage. They often appear in court systems, HR complaints, family disputes, and leadership conflicts. They are the quintessential 'Karens' and 'Chads' we see portrayed on social media.

Not everyone who argues or expresses intense emotion is high-conflict. The difference is frequency, predictability, and inability to de-escalate. The key marker of HCPs is not *occasional* intensity, but a *persistent* pattern of exacerbating conflict, rather than resolving it.

COACH'S INSIGHT

One of my clients was co-parenting with an ex who turned every child drop-off into a public spectacle, with accusations, arguments, and emotional drama. We reframed it: *'You're not there to win the argument — you're there to demonstrate calm leadership to your child, and to set clear boundaries.'* Shifting the goal reduced the client's emotional activation, which in turn made her more effective in handling the conflict.

A client once said, *'I always leave conversations with her (the ex) feeling like I'm the crazy one.'* That's a hallmark of a high-conflict dynamic — confusion, self-doubt, and emotional whiplash.

RESEARCH SPOTLIGHT

Bill Eddy's High Conflict Institute (Eddy, 2011) notes that HCPs consistently show four markers:

    a) all-or-nothing thinking (i.e., rigidity and inflexibility)

    b) unmanaged emotions (i.e., volatile and reactive)

    c) extreme behaviors (i.e., often over-reacting to small slights or barriers)

    d) a persistent focus on blaming others (i.e., lack of accountability and frequent gaslighting). Recognizing these patterns and engaging with an HCP early allows for preventative boundary setting.

CASE STUDY

A high-achieving manager repeatedly clashed with an employee who frequently accused others of sabotage. HR documentation showed a pattern of emotional overreactions, refusal to accept feedback, and threats to escalate. Coaching focused on BIFF communication (brief, informative, friendly, and firm) and setting procedural boundaries rather than trying to mediate emotional distress.

Exercise 50: Conflict Pattern Tracker (Section 11.1)

Journal Prompt:

- Think of someone you suspect may exhibit high-conflict patterns. What specific behaviors have you observed that fit this pattern?

- How have you typically responded? How has that worked (or not worked)?

Exercise:
Create a **Conflict Pattern Tracker**. For one week, note any repeated conflict interactions with this person. Identify themes such as blame, escalation, or emotional volatility.

Conflict Pattern Tracker

Identified Individual: _____

Nature of the relationship: _____

Day of Week	Describe the repeat conflict interactions	Themes (blame, escalation, volatility, etc.)	My Response?	Effectiveness?
Monday				
Tuesday				
Wednesday				
Thursday				
Friday				
Saturday				
Sunday				

11.2 WHY LOGIC AND EMPATHY OFTEN BACKFIRE

In traditional conflict resolution, logic and empathy are useful tools for connection. But with HCPs, these tools can be misused or weaponized. With HCPs, logic feels dismissive, and empathy can reinforce victimhood.

HCPs often use empathy attempts as leverage or distortion, perceiving it as agreement or weakness. Logic can often be twisted to fuel further argument. Attempts to reason with an HCP may lead to circular conversations, accusations, or stonewalling.

The reason? When you use logic with someone operating from a dysregulated emotional state, they may feel unheard or manipulated. Instead, structured statements that avoid emotional content are more effective, as they cool heightened emotion, allowing the HCP to feel safer and less likely to adopt a defensive stance.

Instead of over-explaining or defending, the key is to calmly set limits, redirect the conversation, and stay focused on observable behaviors and boundaries. Nothing works better towards this goal than using the BIFF method outlined in Section 3.2.

Key principle: Stop over-explaining and start setting simple, firm boundaries.

COACH'S INSIGHT

One of my Executive Coaching clients, a C-suite client, continued to engage in back-and-forth email battles with a high-conflict peer. I advised him to try the BIFF method: be Brief, Informative, Friendly, and Firm. His emails went from averaging 4 paragraphs down to 2 sentences. Making this small change removed oxygen from the exchange, and the conflict lost its fuel.

One executive kept emailing long, rational explanations to a hostile board member. It only led to more manipulation. When he switched to brief, factual responses with no emotional content, the drama declined.

RESEARCH SPOTLIGHT

According to research by Goleman (1995; 2006), individuals in a heightened emotional state (amygdala hijack) lose access to rational processing. They often misinterpret logical arguments as dismissive or controlling. HCPs process emotional threat faster than reasoned dialogue; however, the heightened emotions rarely improve their decision-making and ability to dialogue. Emotional regulation must occur first before logical problem-solving can resume.

CASE STUDY

A woman navigating divorce attempted to provide repeated explanations to her husband (now ex-husband) to demonstrate that she wasn't at fault. Her ex-husband used these emails to twist facts in court. Coaching helped her switch to BIFF communication with clear limits and no emotional bait. The result? Her communications were more focused, on point, and omitted a lot of ancillary information that the ex-husband could have used against her.

Exercise 51: The BIFF Method in action (Section 11.2)

Journal Prompt:

- Recall a time you tried to use logic or empathy, and it escalated the conflict.
- What did you say?
- How was it received?

Exercise:

Rewrite your response using the **BIFF method** (see Section 3.2):

- Brief – Informative – Friendly – Firm

_____
_____
_____
_____

Practice delivering your response verbally in the mirror and note emotional shifts in yourself.

11.3. THE 4 TRAITS THAT FUEL HIGH-CONFLICT PATTERNS: H.E.A.R.™

The acronym H.E.A.R.™ captures the common drivers of high-conflict personalities:

- **Hyper-Reactivity:** Minor slights become perceived major attacks, requiring a similar response. Emotional regulation is poor. Their nervous systems live in a fight-or-flight state.

- **Entitlement:** They expect special treatment or immunity from consequences. They believe rules don't apply to them, and that others should make exceptions for them.

- **Allegiance to Victimhood:** Being the victim is a primary identity, used to justify extreme behavior. They thrive on being wronged. Victim identity becomes their source of power.

- **Rigid Thinking:** There is no gray area — people are all good or all bad. Everything is black-or-white. There's no room for nuance or compromise.

Understanding these traits is not about diagnosing — it's about disengaging from the cycle.

COACH'S INSIGHT

In coaching, I often teach clients to name the pattern silently: 'This is H.E.A.R.' Naming it brings awareness to the dynamic at play, diffuses personal attachment, and restores choice.

RESEARCH SPOTLIGHT

Borderline, narcissistic, and paranoid personality features are commonly present in high-conflict behavior patterns (APA DSM-5-TR, 2022). But it's the repeated interactional dynamic, not the label, that matters most.

CASE STUDY

A physician constantly clashed with administrators, claiming persecution. Investigation showed no evidence of wrongdoing, but repeated escalation by the physician himself. Coaching focused on reinforcing behavioral expectations and redirecting emotion toward peer support and resolution rather than institutional blame.

I worked with a divorced dad who tried reasoning with his ex-wife over every holiday schedule. She was demanding the exact schedule she wanted and was inflexible to the changes he requested. Once he understood her entitlement wasn't negotiable, he stopped expecting logic — and focused on structure and setting boundaries.

Exercise 52: H.E.A.R™ Cheat Sheet (Section 11.3)

Journal Prompt:

- Which H.E.A.R.™ traits have you encountered most?

- How do these traits affect your emotional regulation and boundary setting?

Exercise:

Create an H.E.A.R.™ cheat sheet. For each trait (Hyper-Reactivity, Entitlement, Allegiance to Victimhood, Rigid Thinking), write 2 example behaviors and 1 de-escalation response you can practice.

<div align="center">**H.E.A.R.™ cheat sheet**</div>	
Hyper-Reactivity	**Entitlement**
Behavior 1:	Behavior 1:
Behavior 2:	Behavior 2:
Response:	Response:
Allegiance to Victimhood	**Rigid Thinking**
Behavior 1:	Behavior 1:
Behavior 2:	Behavior 2:
Response:	Response:

11.4. HOW TO SET LIMITS WITHOUT ESCALATING THE SITUATION

Limits are not ultimatums — think of them as boundaries plus consequences.

Setting limits with HCPs must be:

- **Clear:** Say what is and is not acceptable. Be clear and brief.
- **Consistent:** Don't change the boundary based on their reaction. Set boundaries to unwanted behaviors, not personality or intention.
- **Neutral:** Avoid language that is shaming, overly-emotional, or justifying.
- **Repetitive:** Expect to reassert boundaries multiple times. Repeat limits without defending them.

Boundaries are not arguments — they are action statements.

> Example: *'If the yelling continues, I will leave the room.'* Then follow through. That's the currency of trust in high-conflict dynamics.

Example: *'I'll continue this conversation if we can keep it respectful. If not, I'll step away.'*

COACH'S INSIGHT

Boundaries are boring by design. When done well, they feel calm, repetitive, and firm. One executive described it as 'taking the drama oxygen out of the room.'

One client implemented a simple mantra: 'Calm, Clear, Consistent.' She used it before every meeting with a volatile coworker. Her stress dropped — and the coworker eventually stopped baiting her.

RESEARCH SPOTLIGHT

Research by Eddy & Ungar (2019) suggests that structured communication protocols — like BIFF (Brief, Informative, Friendly, Firm) — reduce escalations with HCPs by limiting emotional fuel. They found that training professionals in low-emotion, high-structure communication techniques significantly reduced escalation and improved resolution timelines in high-conflict cases.

CASE STUDY

A team lead learned to exit meetings when personal attacks started. Instead of defending, she simply stated, *'We can continue when this conversation is professional.'* Repetition, not argument, shifted the dynamic over time.

Exercise 53: Ready-To-Go Boundary Scripts (Section 11.4)

Journal Prompt:

- What limit or boundary have you struggled to enforce with a difficult person or HCP?
- What fears come up when you think about enforcing it?

Exercise:

Craft 3 boundary scripts using this template:

'When you _____ [behavior],
I will _____ [consequence].'

'When you _____ [behavior],
I will _____ [consequence].'

'When you _____ [behavior],

I will _____ [consequence].'

Practice saying them aloud with calm tone and posture. Reflect on which script feels most empowering.

SECTION 12:

CONFLICT WITH YOURSELF – FROM INNER CRITIC TO INNER PEACE

'Your anxiety is a lying hoe!'
~ **Anonymous**

'It is never too late to be what you might have been.'
~ **George Elliot**

12.1 THE WAR WITHIN: UNDERSTANDING INTERNAL CONFLICT

Internal conflict is the unseen tug-of-war between our beliefs, emotions, and behaviors. It's the dissonance we feel when our values clash with our actions, when our desires oppose our fears, or when our old programming contradicts our current reality. For many high-achievers, the battle is between self-criticism and self-compassion. While external conflicts are visible, internal ones are often silent — yet just as damaging.

For high-achievers, this often manifests as burnout, imposter syndrome, or harsh self-judgment. They may appear confident on the outside but feel like frauds internally. The inner critic whispers, *'You're not enough'*, while the drive for perfection drowns out the need for rest.

Unchecked, internal conflict creates emotional leakage — irritability, overreaction, or withdrawal in relationships. Over time, it reinforces a narrative that we must control everything to feel safe. But real peace is built not through control, but through internal coherence.

Signs of unresolved inner conflict include:

- Rumination and overthinking
- Perfectionism and procrastination

- Self-sabotage in relationships or work

COACH'S INSIGHT

A tech entrepreneur I coached said, *'I feel like I'm sprinting uphill on a treadmill, and still not doing enough.'* He wasn't lazy — he was fragmented. By identifying the critical voice demanding constant motion, we uncovered his fear of becoming obsolete. Naming that fear helped him reclaim his peace.

A client once told me, *'No one's ever been harder on me than me.'* We traced that inner critic to a childhood voice that equated performance with love, stemming from conditional love and affection received by his father. His adult conflicts weren't just about others — they were echoes of an inner war still raging.

RESEARCH SPOTLIGHT

Self-discrepancy theory (Higgins, 1987) describes the distress that arises when our 'actual self' (who we are) is out of sync with our 'ideal self' (who we think we should be). Bridging that gap with compassion rather than punishment is central to emotional well-being.

Research in self-compassion (Neff, 2003) shows that harsh self-judgment increases anxiety, depression, and emotional reactivity — all of which escalate interpersonal conflict. Self-kindness is not weakness; it's psychological leverage.

CASE STUDY

A physician constantly replayed clinical mistakes in his head. He believed self-punishment was the only path to improvement. This pattern stemmed back to harsh criticism from his father as a child and was exacerbated by the tough demands of medical school. Coaching helped him reframe: *'Growth requires accountability — not shame.'* His internal self-talk shifted from *'You're a failure'* to *'What can I learn from this?'*

Exercise 54: Align Your Internal Voice (Section 12.1)

Journal Prompt:

- Identify a recent moment when you felt torn between two internal voices. What did each voice want?
- What deeper belief or fear might have fueled the conflict?

Exercise:

Draw a Venn diagram. In one circle, write the thoughts/feelings of Voice A. In the other, Voice B. In the overlap, write what both parts ultimately want for you. Use this to find internal alignment.

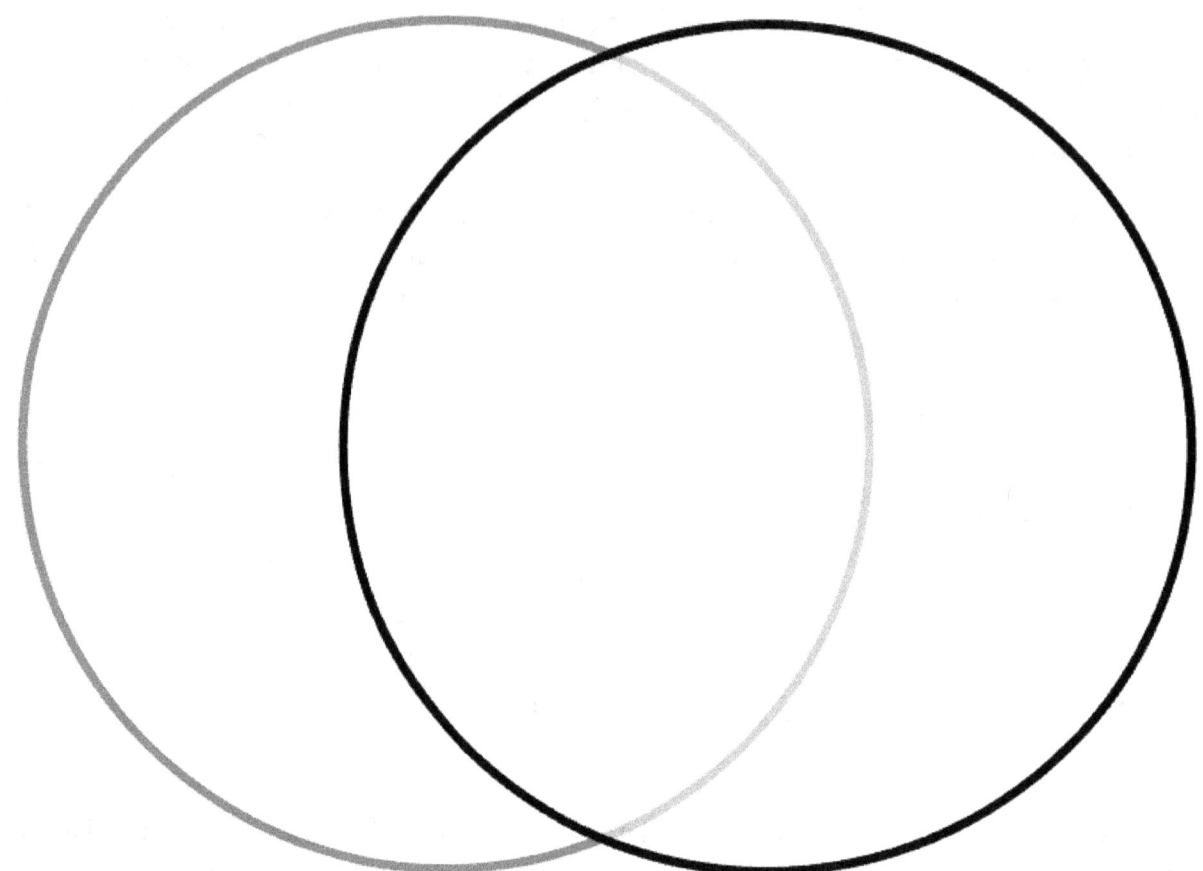

12.2 MEET YOUR INNER CRITIC

The inner critic isn't just negative self-talk. It's a protective part of your psyche that believes criticism will keep you safe — from failure, embarrassment, or rejection.

The inner critic is a voice rooted in survival. It often emerges in childhood as a way to gain approval, avoid punishment, or stay safe. Over time, it becomes internalized as self-monitoring — but when left unchecked, it becomes toxic.

There are several 'subtypes' of the inner critic. Below is a list of these subtypes, as well as the best way to counter each critic's negative voice:

- **The Perfectionist:** Sets impossible standards and shames you for not meeting them.

- **How to counter:** Remind yourself that progress matters more than perfection; aim for 'good enough' rather than flawless.
- **The Taskmaster:** Associates worth with productivity.
  - **How to counter:** Pause and affirm that rest and play fuel productivity — your worth is not tied to output.
- **The Underminer:** Convinces you not to take risks because you're not good enough.
  - **How to counter:** Counter with evidence of past courage and success; taking risks is how growth happens.
- **The Guilt-Tripper:** Weaponizes your conscience/guilt against you.
  - **How to counter:** Reframe guilt by asking, *Is this true responsibility or misplaced shame?* — then act from your values, not fear.
- **The Destroyer:** Attacks your very identity and value.
  - **How to counter:** Respond with self-compassion; separate mistakes from identity and affirm that you are inherently worthy.

While painful, each of these voices developed for a reason. By identifying their function, we can reduce their power and reassign their role. The goal isn't to eliminate the critic — it's to understand its purpose and give it a less damaging job.

COACH'S INSIGHT

A client once said, *'If I talked to my friends the way I talk to myself, I'd have none left.'* That's the litmus test. When we externalize the critic's voice, we hear how cruel it really is — and how undeserved that cruelty always was.

RESEARCH SPOTLIGHT

Neff & Germer (2013) found that self-compassion training reduced levels of self-criticism and increased emotional resilience across diverse populations. The more we understand our inner critic, the more capacity we have to choose a new voice.

According to *Internal Family Systems* (Schwartz, 2001), every inner part, including critics, has a protective function. Lasting change comes from acknowledging, not attacking, those parts.

CASE STUDY

A high-performing executive avoided relationships because his inner voice told him he was *'too intense and broken.'* Through structured journaling and coaching work, he uncovered a scared teenager who had learned to avoid connection after rejection. Healing began when that part felt seen — not silenced.

A high-powered attorney struggled with explosive anger toward colleagues. In coaching, he discovered an inner narrative: *'If I don't dominate, I'll be irrelevant.'* That fear was his critic trying to protect him from past humiliation.

Exercise 55: Your Inner Critic Profile (Section 12.2)

Journal Prompt:

- What does your inner critic say most often?

_____
_____
_____
_____

- Where do you think this voice originated from?

_____
_____
_____
_____

Exercise:

Write a character profile of your inner critic. Give it a name, tone, and backstory. Then write a compassionate letter from your adult self to your inner critic, explaining why this voice can retire — or take a less extreme role in your daily life.

_____
_____

Exercise 55: Your Inner Critic Profile (Section 12.2)

Journal Prompt:

- What does your inner critic say most often?

_____
_____
_____
_____

- Where do you think this voice originated from?

_____
_____
_____
_____

Exercise:

Write a character profile of your inner critic. Give it a name, tone, and backstory. Then write a compassionate letter from your adult self to your inner critic, explaining why this voice can retire — or take a less extreme role in your daily life.

12.3 FROM SELF-JUDGMENT TO SELF-LEADERSHIP

Self-leadership begins with recognizing you are not your thoughts. You are the observer — the 'wise mind' capable of choosing a different internal dialogue.

Self-leadership is the process of becoming the steward of your internal world. It's not about eradicating negative thoughts but becoming less fused to them — creating space between the thought and your identity.

Core practices for developing self-leadership:

- **Awareness:** Notice the inner voice without judgment. What is it trying to say?
- **Dialogue:** Ask what the inner voice is trying to protect you from.
- **Reframe:** Offer a new message from your wiser, adult self.
- **Choice:** Act from alignment to your goals, not from old fear.

This shift changes everything. You move from reacting to leading. From collapse to calm confidence. From 'I must fix myself' to 'I will lead myself.'

This reframe allows internal conflict to shift from war to dialogue — the foundation for peace.

COACH'S INSIGHT

I tell clients: The voice that says, *'What's wrong with you?'* is not your truth. The truth is quieter, kinder, and infinitely wiser. You've just practiced the other voice longer. It's time to change the station.

I teach clients to write a dialogue between their critic and their inner leader. Once written, the harshness loses power. The leader always ends the conversation — calm, clear, and compassionate.

RESEARCH SPOTLIGHT

Mindfulness-based practices improve meta-cognition — the ability to observe thoughts without buying into them wholesale or adopting them without question. This decreases emotional reactivity and improves conflict management. Kabat-Zinn's (1994) work on mindfulness reveals that the act of observing thoughts without judgment changes our relationship to them. When we no longer believe every thought, we are free to respond from choice, not compulsion.

CASE STUDY

A nurse practitioner struggled with burnout and guilt, working excessive hours with difficult patients. Her inner critic told her she was selfish for setting boundaries. We role-played her critic and inner leader in session. Eventually, her leader's voice — calm, strong, clear — became louder than the shame.

Exercise 56: Your Inner Critic Dialogue (Section 12.3)

Journal Prompt:

- Describe a time you led yourself through a difficult moment instead of reacting impulsively. What helped you access that leader energy?

Exercise:

Dialogue writing:

- On one side, write what your inner critic said, or would say.
- On the other side, write what your balanced self would say

Your Inner Critic Voice	Your Balanced Self Voice

SECTION 13:

REPAIRING THE RELATIONSHIP WITH YOURSELF

'We repeat what we do not repair.'
~ **Anonymous**

'The wound is the place where the Light enters you.'
~ **Rumi**

13.1 THE RUPTURE WITHIN: WHY WE TURN AGAINST OURSELVES

When conflict strikes, most people think of the tension between two people. But often, the longest war we fight is internal. This rupture within—between our values and actions, between self-awareness and shame—is where many breakdowns begin. One of the most painful outcomes of unresolved conflict isn't just losing a relationship—it's losing trust in yourself.

Psychologists refer to this as 'intrapersonal conflict.' It can manifest as chronic indecision, intense self-doubt, emotional numbness, or imposter syndrome. These inner battles are exhausting, eroding our confidence and causing us to disconnect not only from others, but from ourselves.

High-achievers often internalize conflict by self-blaming, bringing out their internal critic: *'I should've known better'*, or *'Why did I stay so long?'* This spirals into shame, self-doubt, and avoidance. The result? A fractured relationship with the self.

The internal critic often emerges as a coping mechanism—an attempt to avoid future pain by being hyper-vigilant or perfectionistic. But over time, it becomes a source of paralysis. Healing this rupture means naming it, validating it, and choosing to relate to yourself with honesty and care rather than contempt.

Self-rupture shows up in many ways:

- You struggle to make decisions, second-guessing everything.
- You numb out with overwork or distraction.
- You isolate, convinced no one can really understand.

But here's the truth: conflict with yourself is often the root of conflict with others. Repair starts when you stop fighting yourself and start listening instead.

COACH'S INSIGHT

I once worked with a divorced physician who said, *'I feel like I abandoned myself in that marriage.'* That clarity helped him realize healing wasn't just about moving on—it was about reconnecting with the version of himself he betrayed.

A high-performing client once said, *'I never had to worry about conflict with others because I was too busy fighting myself.'* We worked to identify that his inner critic was his father's voice, internalized from childhood. Once he began to separate his present self from that critical echo, he was able to lead himself with more compassion and clarity.

RESEARCH SPOTLIGHT

Self-repair is strongly linked to self-compassion. Neff & Germer (2013) found that people who cultivate self-kindness recover faster from emotional wounds and display greater resilience in relationships.

According to Baumeister et al. (1994), individuals experiencing unresolved internal conflict expend significant mental and emotional resources, leading to burnout and reduced relational resilience. The ability to integrate competing parts of the self is a hallmark of emotional intelligence.

Exercise 57: Your Critic vs Advocate vs. Grounded Self Dialogue (Section 13.1)

Journal Prompt:

- Reflect on a time you felt torn between two conflicting parts of yourself. What were those parts trying to protect?
- How did your internal critic influence your external behavior?

Exercise:

Create a dialogue between your 'inner critic' and your 'inner advocate'. Let each have a voice. Notice the tone, needs, and fears behind each.

Conclude with a third voice—your grounded, adult self—summarizing what you've learned and what comes next.

Your Inner Critic (tone, needs, fears)	Your Inner Advocate (tone, needs, fears)	Your Grounded Voice (learnings, what next?)

13.2 THE POWER OF SELF-FORGIVENESS

Self-forgiveness is one of the most powerful forms of emotional release—and also one of the most misunderstood. Self-forgiveness isn't about letting yourself off the hook—it's about releasing yourself from the endless punishment loop.

Forgiving yourself doesn't mean minimizing harm or excusing behavior. It means acknowledging your humanity and choosing to heal, rather than endlessly punish yourself.

The process of self-forgiveness includes: Acknowledging harm (to yourself or others)

- Taking responsibility without over-identifying with guilt
- Repairing where possible—and releasing what's not yours to carry

The four Rs of self-forgiveness:

1. **Responsibility:** owning your part with honesty
2. **Remorse:** experiencing sincere regret
3. **Repair:** taking action to make amends (when possible)
4. **Release:** letting go of self-condemnation to move forward

Without self-forgiveness, we stay stuck in cycles of sabotage or overcompensation. With it, we begin to access growth, clarity, and peace.

You don't need to be perfect to be worthy of peace. Forgiveness says: *'I'm allowed to be human and still grow.'*

COACH'S INSIGHT

Self-forgiveness is a decision – a decision that you make and follow through on daily. Forgiveness is not feeling. It has feelings associated with it – some days those are good feelings, some days those are bad feelings. But the decision to forgive ourselves is indeed a decision we make, and the ups and downs of our feelings should not alter our commitment. On bad days when feeling down, we navigate through those uncomfortable feelings, but the self-forgiveness remains steady.

RESEARCH SPOTLIGHT

Enright et al. (2000) demonstrated that self-forgiveness interventions significantly reduce anxiety, anger, and depression—key emotions that fuel interpersonal conflict and inhibit healing.

In a 2015 meta-analysis published in the *Journal of Counseling Psychology*, researchers found that self-forgiveness is strongly correlated with reduced depressive symptoms, greater relationship satisfaction, and increased likelihood of behavior change (Davis et al., 2015).

CASE STUDY

A tech founder who lost his marriage after prioritizing work over family was haunted by guilt. In coaching, he explored the roots of his behavior—his identity was tied to performance, to his success. Through self-forgiveness exercises, he learned to separate his inherent self-worth from his productivity, allowing him to re-engage with his children with presence and peace.

A high-level executive carried deep guilt for abandoning his family during a years-long affair. Through guided self-forgiveness work, he wrote letters to each version of himself—the betrayer, the ashamed, the wounded. The result wasn't erasing the past but reclaiming his future.

Exercise 58: Letter of Self-Forgiveness (Section 13.2)

Journal Prompt:

- What do you most need to forgive yourself for?
- What would change in your life if you released this burden?

Exercise:

Write a letter of self-forgiveness. Use the four R's: **Responsibility, Remorse, Repair, Release**.

Read the letter aloud to yourself in a mirror. Then, seal it in an envelope labeled: 'I forgive myself. This stays in the past.'

13.3 REBUILDING TRUST IN YOUR OWN DECISION-MAKING

After ruptures, many people lose confidence in their ability to choose wisely. They ask, *'How can I ever trust myself again?'* This erosion of self-trust shows up as hesitation, anxiety, and reliance on external validation.

Rebuilding self-trust requires a slow and steady return to internal alignment.

This involves:

- Reviewing past choices with curiosity:
- Were your choices aligned with your values, or based in fear?
- Tracking small wins:
- Even micro-decisions (choosing rest, honoring boundaries) restore inner confidence.
- Using values as a compass rather than fear:
- Let your decisions reflect who you are—not what others expect.

Self-trust isn't about being right—it's about being in right relationship with yourself.

COACH'S INSIGHT

I teach clients to build 'micro-habits of trust' – keeping promises to themselves, setting boundaries, or choosing rest, and doing so in small ways that build momentum. These rebuild confidence from the inside out.

I often assign clients a 'trust journal' where they write down every time they keep a promise to themselves. Over time, this practice rebuilds inner credibility—an antidote to chronic self-doubt.

RESEARCH SPOTLIGHT

According to Rotenberg (2010), the foundation of self-trust involves congruence between thoughts, feelings, and behaviors. When internal alignment is strengthened, decision-making becomes more efficient and emotionally grounded.

Exercise 59: Micro-Moments of Trust Log (Section 13.3)

Journal Prompt:

- Where in your life do you currently hesitate to trust yourself?
- When was the last time you kept a promise to yourself?

Exercise:

Start a 'Micro-Moments of Trust' log.

Each day for 1 week, write down one small way you showed up for yourself: made a decision, honored a boundary, practiced self-respect, etc.

Day of Week	How did I show up for Myself?
Monday	
Tuesday	
Wednesday	
Thursday	
Friday	
Saturday	
Sunday	

13.4 CULTIVATING INNER SAFETY AND INTEGRITY

At the core of every conflict is one question: *'Am I safe being fully myself here?'*

If the answer is no, we perform, contort, or disappear. When conflict erodes us from the inside, our nervous system often stays in a chronic state of threat.

Cultivating inner safety is about creating a psychological space where all parts of you feel welcomed—not judged. To truly repair, you must create a sanctuary within—where your thoughts, needs, and emotions are welcomed.

Steps to cultivate inner safety:

- Create internal boundaries (no shame spiraling past 10 minutes, limiting rumination)
- Daily self-regulation (breathing, grounding, movement)
- Self-validation (Speak to yourself with the tone you'd use with someone you love)
- Replace *'What's wrong with me?'* with *'What's needing attention here?'*

Inner integrity means aligning your outer choices with your inner truth. It allows you to live with dignity, even when things fall apart. When you lead yourself from this space, you become less reactive and more anchored in conflict with others. The more congruent you are, the less internal conflict you carry.

COACH'S INSIGHT

When self-doubt enters, replace *'What's **wrong** with me?'* with *'What's **Strong** with me?'*

RESEARCH SPOTLIGHT

Brené Brown (2012) notes that shame thrives in secrecy but dissolves in empathy. Inner safety allows us to witness our own imperfections without turning against ourselves.

Porges' *Polyvagal Theory* highlights that perceived safety—especially internal safety—is essential for emotional regulation and social connection. Without it, individuals remain in a state of hypervigilance or shutdown (Porges, 2011).

CASE STUDY

A burnt-out corporate manager said, *'I've spent 15 years living up to expectations I never agreed to.'* We worked to identify her authentic values and began a process of reclaiming her voice—first in private, then in her professional role.

A healthcare leader experiencing panic attacks discovered that she'd been living out of alignment for years—pleasing everyone but herself. We focused on reconnecting her to her core values and boundaries. Once she honored those, the panic subsided; she felt more 'at home' in her own body.

Exercise 60: The Integrity Inventory (Section 13.4)

Journal Prompt:

- What does 'feeling safe inside' mean to you?
- Where do you currently feel out of alignment between your inner truth and outer behavior?

Exercise:

Create an 'Integrity Inventory':

- List 5 current behaviors that reflect your values.

- List 3 that don't.

Choose one small change you'll make this week to bring yourself closer to aligning your behaviors with your values. Repeat this exercise when you are feeling out of integrity with your values and priorities.

5 Behaviors that Reflect My Values	3 Behaviors that do NOT
1	1
2	2
3	3
4	
5	
What change am I committing to this week? _____ _____ _____	

SECTION 14:
CREATING A CONFLICT-RESILIENT LIFE

'We are the music makers, and the dreamers of dreams.'
~ Willy Wonka

'Fate whispers to the warrior, 'You cannot withstand the storm.' The warrior whispers back, 'I am the storm."
~ Folk Proverb

14.1 WHAT IS A CONFLICT-RESILIENT LIFE?

A conflict-resilient life is not one without conflict—it's a life in which conflict is met with skill, clarity, and care. It's one where you anticipate, navigate, and bounce back from conflict with balance and confidence. Instead of fearing rupture, you expect it, prepare for it, and know how to move through it. It's the ability to stay emotionally grounded, communicatively skilled, and values-aligned even when things get hard.

The goal isn't to eliminate conflict. That's unrealistic and, frankly, unhealthy. Conflict is a signal – of change, of need, of misalignment. When you become fluent in responding to those signals, you stop fearing conflict and start using it as a tool for connection and growth.

Resilience in conflict means:

- You recover faster from emotional triggers
- You no longer fear difficult conversations
- You know how to hold both strength and empathy

A conflict-resilient life reflects three principles:

1. Responsiveness over reactivity

2. Proactive repair instead of avoidance
3. Inner regulation before outer reaction

Most people try to design a life where conflict won't happen. But real mastery means building a nervous system, mindset, and environment where conflict doesn't derail you.

It's a nervous system that knows how to settle. A mindset that knows how to reflect. And a lifestyle that gives you space to recalibrate before you explode, withdraw, or collapse.

COACH'S INSIGHT

One of my executive clients once said, *'I used to dread every team meeting because I knew conflict would arise. Now, I lean into it because I know who I am inside it, and I know how to manage it.'* That's the shift we're aiming for—ownership, not avoidance.

In my executive coaching work, I've seen people lead global teams with confidence, but melt down in one text argument with a partner. Why? Because they never learned to extend their leadership to their inner world. Conflict resilience isn't just a skillset—it's a self-leadership stance. It's the belief: *'I can stay with myself no matter how hot the moment gets.'*

RESEARCH SPOTLIGHT

Tugade and Fredrickson's (2004) research on resilience shows that individuals who regularly use positive emotions and reflective coping strategies recover more quickly from stress, have better relationship outcomes, and experience fewer chronic health conditions. Further, resilience is associated with greater emotional regulation and cognitive reappraisal during stress—both essential in managing interpersonal conflict effectively.

CASE STUDY

A high-powered attorney came to coaching after a series of angry outbursts with staff and her partner. She felt emotionally hijacked by conflict. We worked on recognizing her escalation cues and building a 3-step recovery plan: pause, regulate, reflect. Within 2 months, her reactivity dropped by 70%, and her team began trusting her leadership again.

Exercise 61: Your Resilience Map (Section 14.1)

Journal Prompt:

- What does a conflict-resilient version of your life look like?
- Where do you currently feel most emotionally reactive?

- What relationships or environments challenge your regulation the most?

Exercise:

Draw a **Resilience Map**. Identify key daily, weekly, and monthly practices you can put in place to support your emotional balance (e.g., morning grounding, weekly repair talks, solo reflection time).

Daily	Weekly	Monthly
_____	_____	_____
_____	_____	_____
_____	_____	_____
_____	_____	_____
_____	_____	_____
_____	_____	_____
_____	_____	_____

14.2 INTEGRATING CONFLICT SKILLS INTO EVERYDAY LIFE

Conflict resilience isn't a 'when-it-happens' skill—it's a lifestyle. To create long-term transformation, your conflict approach must be embedded in your daily relationships, habits, and systems.

Many people try to 'use conflict tools' only when things are already falling apart. But by then, the nervous system is flooded and logic is offline. The best time to use conflict tools? Daily. Preventatively.

Here's how integration looks:

- Weekly family or team check-ins with open feedback, where everyone names tensions or needs before they explode.

- Practicing micro-validation in conversations – 'I hear you'; 'I see you'.

- Daily Regulation – Breathwork, body scans, or movement to clear emotional charge. Catching and naming your triggers early.

- Rebuilding faster after arguments through mini-scripts – phrases like *'Can we pause?'* or *'I want to get this right'* become habitual rather than forced.

This isn't about perfection—it's about fluency. When conflict becomes a normal part of growth, it loses its power to dominate you.

COACH'S INSIGHT

One couple I worked with committed to 15-minute 'Connection & Conflict' check-ins twice a week. At first, it felt awkward. But within 6 weeks, they had fewer blowouts and more closeness. Integration is about rhythm, not perfection.

RESEARCH SPOTLIGHT

Gottman Institute research (Gottman & Levenson, 1999) shows that the ratio of positive to negative interactions in relationships must be at least 5:1 to maintain emotional connection: 5 positive interactions for every single negative interaction. Regular integration of conflict-resolution skills sustains this balance and reduces long-term relational volatility.

CASE STUDY

A senior sales executive began using validation scripts in his Monday meetings – *'I see the hard work you're putting in'*; *'I hear your concerns, and I'm taking them seriously'*; *'I appreciate the effort you made on this last project'*. His team—once defensive and silent—started opening up. Performance improved, but more importantly, trust was rebuilt. Integration created a ripple effect across the culture.

A couple I coached decided to implement a 'Sunday Reset Board Meeting'—30 minutes each week to discuss wins, unmet needs, and repair any friction. Over time, this single practice reduced the intensity of their fights by more than half and created emotional safety for both partners.

Exercise 62: 7-Day Habit Practice (Section 14.2)

Journal Prompt:

- When are you most likely to avoid conflict?

- What's one micro-skill (validation, pausing, naming need) you can use today?

Exercise:

Choose one habit from this workbook (e.g., the V.E.N.T. Method, validation, curiosity) and commit to practicing it for 7 days in real interactions.

At the end of each day, journal:

- What went well?

_____

_____

- What was hard?

_____

_____

- What shifted as a result?

_____

_____

14.3 SYSTEMS THAT SUPPORT EMOTIONAL SUSTAINABILITY

You cannot sustain emotional resilience without support. High performers burn out when they treat emotional regulation as an afterthought. Even the most skilled communicators burn out without support. Emotional sustainability means having routines, relationships, and boundaries that protect your capacity. Emotional sustainability is about proactive, non-negotiable systems that protect your energy.

Key Pillars of Emotional Sustainability:

- **Daily Reset Rituals:** Daily regulation rituals (e.g., breathwork, journaling, nature walks). Morning or evening routines (movement, breathwork, intention setting) that anchor the nervous system.
- **Recovery Zones:** Time blocks or spaces in your day that allow for emotional decompression (e.g., no back-to-back meetings).

- **Reflective Practice:** Weekly journaling, coaching, or therapy to debrief emotions and grow through patterns.
- **Emotional First Responders:** Develop a support ecosystem, one or two trusted people you can call when spiraling—without judgment.
- **Clear Boundaries:** Setting clear limits around toxic dynamics or information overload

Without these systems, conflict will erode your presence, performance, and peace. Conflict is depleting. Resilience requires rest and reinforcement. You cannot be your best self in conflict if you are emotionally bankrupt.

COACH'S INSIGHT

Many high performers treat emotional health like a luxury. But conflict exposure is inevitable. I tell clients: If you're not actively restoring your emotional energy, you're unconsciously leaking it into your relationships.

I have my executive clients schedule 'EQ Workouts'—10-minute emotional fitness routines that include breathing, naming what they feel, and aligning with purpose and intention. Just like physical fitness, emotional stamina is built through reps.

RESEARCH SPOTLIGHT

The concept of 'allostatic load' describes how accumulated stress from unresolved emotional strain damages physical and psychological health. Research by McEwen & Gianaros (2010) on allostatic load reveals that chronic emotional stress—especially unresolved conflict—wears down the body's regulatory systems. Sustainable routines and safe relationships act as buffers to that wear.

CASE STUDY

A high-growth startup founder was facing burnout. We mapped out a 5-day cycle of emotional hygiene: solo walks, Friday reflection rituals, and mid-day transitions. He reported sharper focus, fewer emotional outbursts, and a 40% drop in perceived stress.

Exercise 63: Emotional Drains vs. Emotional Supports (Section 14.3)

Journal Prompt:

- What drains you emotionally the most right now?
- What fills your emotional cup?

- Where are your current gaps in recovery or support?

Exercise:

Create a two-column chart:

Column 1: 'Emotional Drains' – list 5 common stressors or patterns.

Column 2: 'Emotional Supports' – list current or potential rituals, people, and boundaries that replenish you.

Choose one new support to schedule into your week immediately.

Emotional Drains **5 Common Stressors/Patterns**	**Emotional Supports** **Current/Potential rituals, people, boundaries**
1 2 3 4 5	1 2 3 4 5

Which new support will you incorporate into your week?

_____

_____

_____

SECTION 15:
FROM CONFLICT TO GROWTH

'Between stimulus and response there is a space. In that space is our power to choose our response. In our response lies our growth and our freedom.'
~ Viktor Frankl

Conflict doesn't have to be a destructive force. Think of conflict as the laboratory of transformation. When you learn to navigate it with clarity, self-respect, and empathy, it becomes a forge — transforming raw emotion into stronger relationships, sharper leadership, and deeper self-awareness.

Every difficult conversation, every rupture, every misunderstanding is an invitation to decide: Will you repeat the same cycle, or will you grow? The five areas in this chapter take you beyond 'managing' conflict into using it as a catalyst for personal power, relational trust, and lasting change.

This chapter explores how to move from the heat of disagreement into the light of growth.

15.1 BOUNDARIES: THE LOVE LANGUAGE OF SELF-RESPECT

Boundaries are not walls; they are doors with handles you control. They signal to others how to treat you, and they teach you to treat yourself with dignity. Without them, conflict becomes a game of erosion — every argument eats away at your sense of self.

Healthy boundaries are not about pushing people away — they're about protecting your capacity to stay connected without resentment. They tell others, *'I know where I end and you begin.'* In relationships without boundaries, conflict becomes either constant power struggles or quiet emotional erosion.

Boundaries can be:

- Physical – *'I need space right now'*
- Emotional – *'I won't accept being spoken to that way'*
- Time-based – *'I can meet with you, but only for 30 minutes'*.

When you're clear, you stop leaving others to guess — and stop resenting them when they guess wrong.

COACH'S INSIGHT

When clients tell me they *'don't want to make a big deal'* about something, I remind them: *'The moment you feel resentful, you've already made it a big deal — just silently.'* Boundaries set early are easier to hold than boundaries set after you've reached a breaking point.

I often see high-achievers treat boundaries like luxury items — *'I'll set them when things calm down.'* But boundaries are *why* things calm down. Without them, your relationships run on hope and endurance, not clarity and respect.

RESEARCH SPOTLIGHT

A 2017 study published in *Frontiers in Psychology, Nie and colleagues* found that individuals with clear personal boundaries reported lower stress levels, less anxiety, higher relationship satisfaction, greater self-esteem, and better conflict resolution outcomes. Boundaries act as a protective buffer, reducing emotional reactivity — they protect the relationship by reducing friction.

CASE STUDY

A high-achieving executive was burning out because she said yes to every request. In coaching, we scripted three assertive but warm 'boundary statements' she could use. The first week she used them, she cut her meeting load by 25% — and no one thought less of her.

A senior VP was constantly 'on call' for her CEO. Through coaching, she drafted a new communication agreement: no non-urgent texts after 8 p.m., and all weekend requests went through her assistant. Initially nervous about pushback, she was shocked when the CEO respected it immediately — and even thanked her for modeling healthy leadership.

Exercise 64: Your Boundary Audit (Section 15.1)

- Boundary Audit: List three areas in your life where you often feel drained or resentful.

1. _____
2. _____
3. _____

What boundary could prevent this?

_____

_____

- Practice Script: Write and rehearse one boundary statement for a personal relationship and one for a professional relationship.

- Journal Prompt: How has your relationship to boundaries changed over time, and what do you want it to look like moving forward?

15.2 FORGIVENESS WITHOUT CLOSURE: RELEASING WHAT HURTS

Forgiveness without closure is one of the most misunderstood concepts in conflict work. Many believe they *can't* forgive until the other person admits fault. But waiting for that apology is like waiting for rain in the desert — your peace remains hostage to their capacity (or willingness) to change.

Sometimes you'll never get the apology, the explanation, or the justice you deserve. Waiting for it traps you in the very dynamic you want to escape. Forgiveness without closure is not pretending it didn't happen — it's reclaiming your peace without their participation.

This isn't about excusing harmful behavior. It's about choosing not to carry it anymore. When you forgive without closure, you close the loop *inside yourself*. That act frees you to live without replaying the injury.

COACH'S INSIGHT

Closure is not an external event; it's an internal decision. You can release resentment and still acknowledge the wrong. Forgiveness is a boundary too — it's saying, '*You no longer get to occupy my emotional real estate.*'

I tell clients: '*Forgiveness doesn't require reconciliation. You can forgive from a distance — and sometimes that's the only healthy option.*'

RESEARCH SPOTLIGHT

Dr. Everett Worthington's REACH Forgiveness model shows that forgiving, even in the absence of closure, reduces stress hormones, improves cardiovascular health, and increases psychological well-being. Forgiveness improves mental health and reduces symptoms of depression, even when the offending party doesn't participate. Neuroimaging reveals decreased amygdala activity — the brain's 'threat center' — when practicing forgiveness.

CASE STUDY

One client was waiting for his estranged brother to admit fault for a family business betrayal. After years of silence, he decided to 'close the loop' himself by writing a letter he never sent. He felt lighter in a week than he had in a decade.

A client's business partner embezzled funds, then disappeared without acknowledgment. Years of bitterness kept the client stuck. Through coaching, he wrote an unsent letter acknowledging the harm and formally releasing the anger. He later told me, *'I didn't get justice, but I got my peace and myself back.'*

Exercise 65: The Letter of Release (Section 15.2)

- Letter of Release: Write a letter to someone you're ready to forgive (you don't have to send it). State the harm, acknowledge your feelings, and release them.

- Self-Check: Identify one resentment you've been holding:

  _____

  _____

  What does it cost you emotionally, mentally, and physically?

  _____

  _____

  _____

  _____

- Journal Prompt: How would your life feel different if you forgave without needing their participation?

15.3 CREATING A CONFLICT CULTURE: WITH FAMILY, TEAMS, PARTNERS

Conflict culture is the invisible rulebook of how disagreement happens in your family, team, or partnership. Some cultures allow open dialogue; others punish it. In unhealthy cultures, conflict is either explosive and personal, or avoided at all costs — which only delays the explosion.

Families, teams, and couples all have 'unwritten rules' about conflict — who gets loud, who goes silent, who gets the last word. These rules become the culture. Healthy conflict cultures make it safe to disagree, voice needs, and repair.

Shifting the culture requires intentional modeling. It's not just about 'how we argue,' but 'how we repair.' Healthy cultures make it safe to bring tension to the surface without fear of retaliation, ridicule, or rejection.

COACH'S INSIGHT

The leader sets the tone — whether that's the CEO in a company, the parent in a home, or the emotionally mature partner in a couple. If you react with blame, you train people to hide. If you respond with curiosity, you train people to speak.

The leader — whether that's the manager, parent, or partner with more emotional stability — sets the tone. If you normalize calm, curiosity, and repair, the culture will follow.

RESEARCH SPOTLIGHT

Google's *Project Aristotle* (Rozovsky, 2015) found that psychological safety was the single most important predictor of team effectiveness. Similar research in family therapy shows that children raised in emotionally safe households with open emotional dialogue develop stronger problem-solving skills and better resilience in adulthood.

CASE STUDY

A blended family constantly erupted at the dinner table. Through coaching, they introduced a pause phrase — *'reset'* — anyone could say to stop escalation. At first awkward, it became a ritual of mutual respect. Conflicts still happened, but blowups decreased by over 60% in two months.

Exercise 66: Your Culture Map & Reset Ritual (Section 15.3)

- Culture Mapping: Describe your family, team, or partnership's current conflict culture. Identify at least two norms that need shifting.

Current Conflict Culture	2 Norms that need Shifting
	1. _____ 2. _____

- Reset Ritual: Create a 'pause phrase' you can introduce to help de-escalate conflict. Practice using it in a low-stakes conversation.

    Pause Phrase:

    _____

- Journal Prompt: What would a healthy conflict culture look like in your life, and what role will you play in creating it?

    _____

    _____

15.4 CONFLICT AS INTIMACY, GROWTH, AND LEADERSHIP

When conflict is navigated with skill, it becomes a form of intimacy. Handled well, conflict deepens trust. The act of surviving a disagreement and coming out stronger signals that the relationship is durable — that it can hold both connection and difference.

You're showing the other person, *'I trust you enough to bring you my truth, even when it's uncomfortable.'* In leadership, it signals strength — not the absence of disagreement, but the ability to harness it.

True intimacy and strong leadership are built on trust that the relationship can hold disagreement without breaking. Avoidance undermines that trust; skillful engagement reinforces it.

COACH'S INSIGHT

In leadership and love alike, conflict is a proving ground. How you show up in disagreement tells people whether they can trust you when things get hard. Avoidance breeds fragility; skillful engagement breeds resilience.

People often say, *'I don't like conflict.'* What they really mean is, *'I don't like the way I've experienced conflict.'* When you redefine it as a connection through truth-telling, it stops being a threat and starts being a resource.

RESEARCH SPOTLIGHT

A *Journal of Applied Psychology* (DeDreu & Weingart, 2003) meta-analysis found that 'constructive conflict' in teams — where members challenge ideas but maintain respect — is linked to higher innovation and problem-solving capacity.

In intimate relationships, Dr. John Gottman's research (Gottman & Silver, 1999) shows that couples who repair quickly after conflict are the ones most likely to thrive long-term.

CASE STUDY

A CEO I worked with was known for shutting down dissent. After adopting 'conflict curiosity' as a leadership value, she started inviting team members to 'poke holes' in her ideas.

Not only did morale improve, but revenue grew 15% from better decision-making and increased innovation.

Another CEO avoided disagreements with her COO to 'keep the peace.' This created costly blind spots. With coaching, she began holding monthly 'friction forums' where they discussed emerging tensions openly. Within six months, team productivity improved, and the COO later said it was the healthiest professional relationship he'd ever had.

Exercise 67: Intimacy & Leadership Conflict Inventory (Section 15.4)

- Intimacy Inventory: List three relationships where conflict has strengthened trust. What made the difference?

    Relationship 1:

    _____

    _____

    The Difference?

    _____

    _____

    Relationship 2:

    _____

    _____

    The Difference?

    _____

    _____

    Relationship 3:

    _____

    _____

The Difference?

_____

_____

- Leadership Reflection: Think of a leader you trust. How do they handle conflict, and how can you model that?

    Leader:

    _____

    _____

    Their conflict style/approach:

    _____

    _____

- Journal Prompt: How can you redefine conflict as a tool for connection rather than a threat to it?

    _____

    _____

    _____

15.5 BUILDING YOUR PERSONAL CONFLICT PLAYBOOK

No athlete goes into a game without a playbook — and no leader or partner should go into conflict without one either. A personal conflict playbook gives you repeatable scripts, grounding techniques, and repair rituals you can deploy under stress.

A conflict playbook is your custom toolkit — scripts, strategies, grounding practices, and repair rituals — ready for when emotions run high. Without one, you default to old habits (avoidance, attack, shutdown) that keep the cycle going.

The best playbooks include:

- **Proactive tools** for initiating tough conversations.
- **Reactive tools** for self-regulation when triggered.
- **Repair rituals** to restore connection afterward.
- **A Roadmap** for navigating and redirecting conflict

As you build your playbook, reflect on the conflict roadmap (flowchart) below to recognize the stages of possible conflict escalation, as well as the optimal response technique or approach to use at each stage.

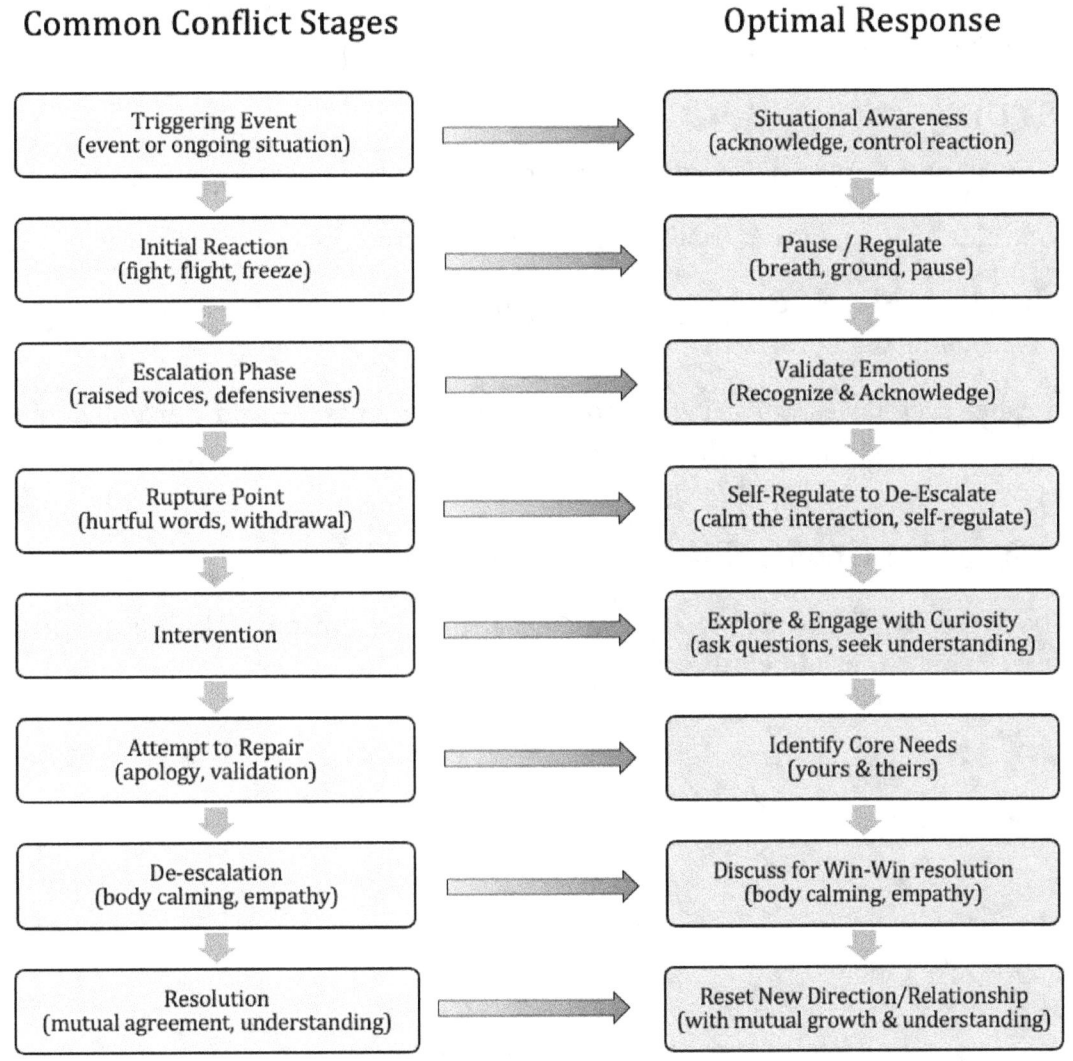

COACH'S INSIGHT

Your playbook should include both 'Offense' tools (how to initiate a tough conversation) and 'Defense' tools (how to de-escalate when you're triggered). Without it, you'll rely on instinct — which is usually your worst habits in disguise.

Think of your playbook as a fire drill for your relationships. You don't wait for a building to burn to decide how to evacuate — you practice in advance so you can respond quickly and well under pressure.

RESEARCH SPOTLIGHT

Self-regulation studies by Driskell and colleagues (1994) show that pre-rehearsed coping scripts increase constructive engagement by 50% compared to reacting in the moment. Mental rehearsal activates the same neural pathways as real-life performance, improving response under stress.

CASE STUDY

One senior manager created a 'conflict card' she kept in her notebook.

    On one side → grounding tools to use when triggered (i.e., calming breath techniques)

    On the other → open-ended questions to invite dialogue (i.e., *What do you most need from me right now?*').

It became her secret weapon in tense boardroom moments — and her colleagues began seeking her out as a conflict mediator, eventually earning her a promotion.

Exercise 68: Your Conflict Playbook (Section 15.5)

- Playbook Draft: Write down 3 proactive scripts, 3 calming techniques, and 2 repair strategies you can use in conflict.

3 Proactive Scripts	3 Calming Techniques	2 Repair Strategies
1 _____ _____ _____ _____	1 _____ _____ _____ _____	1 _____ _____ _____ _____
2 _____ _____ _____ _____	2 _____ _____ _____ _____	2 _____ _____ _____ _____
3 _____ _____ _____ _____	3 _____ _____ _____ _____	

- Mental Rehearsal: Choose one script from your playbook and practice it aloud until it feels natural.

- Journal Prompt: How will having a conflict playbook change your confidence and clarity in difficult situations?

SECTION 16:

THE CONFLICT WHISPERER'S TOOLKIT

'Difficulties mastered are opportunities won.'
~ Winston Churchill

16.1 QUICK-REFERENCE SCRIPTS: COMMUNICATION ON THE FRONT LINES

When you're flooded or defensive, access to language narrows. Quick-reference scripts serve as verbal grounding tools—they provide structure during emotionally unpredictable moments.

These short, direct, and grounded phrases help center the conversation:

Validation Examples:

- *'That makes sense. I didn't see it that way before.'*
- *'I can hear that this matters a lot to you.'*

Curious Questions:

- *'Can you walk me through what that was like for you?'*
- *'What did you need from me in that moment?'*

Boundary Scripts:

- *'I want to talk about this, but not while we're yelling.'*
- *'It's okay for us to disagree, but not to disrespect.'*

Use these as scaffolding. Over time, you'll adapt them to your own voice.

COACH'S INSIGHT

After weeks of explosive fights, one client in couples therapy began using a simple validation line to their partner, *'I hear you and I want to understand you better'*. That sentence changed the tone of their dynamic in under a week.

RESEARCH SPOTLIGHT

Gottman Institute findings (Gottman & Levenson, 1999) show that turning toward instead of away—especially with simple, validating language—predicts long-term relational success by up to 80%.

CASE STUDY

A senior manager applied validation scripts in performance reviews, shifting from critique to curiosity, and seeking understanding and clarity before judgment. Employee morale improved, and HR noted a sharp drop in complaints about tone.

Exercise 69: Practice Quick-Reference Scripts (Section 16.1)

Choose 2–3 of the quick-reference scripts from above (Section 16.1)

- Practice saying them out loud in front of a mirror.
- Then try them in a real conversation this week.
- Journal: What felt awkward? What felt surprisingly effective?
- Which scripts feel most natural to you? Which feel like a stretch?

16.2 YOUR GO-TO EMERGENCY DE-ESCALATION STRATEGIES

Sometimes things get heated fast. In the heat of conflict, your prefrontal cortex goes offline. To help interrupt that spiral, these tools help you interrupt the escalation and steer toward regulation and repair.

The 90-Second Reset: Based on neuroscientific research, strong emotions physically pass through the body in 90 seconds—unless we re-trigger them. Step away, breathe slowly, and focus on physically grounding yourself (touch a surface, feel your feet, do the '5-4-3-2-1 method' from Section 2.3). This creates space for the prefrontal cortex to re-engage.

Name It to Tame It: UCLA neuroscientist Dan Siegel's technique for reducing amygdala activation. Simply labeling the feeling calms the brain. Say out loud: *'I'm getting defensive right now. Let me pause.'* Naming your state reduces its power.

Postpone with Intention: Avoiding conflict breeds resentment. Postponing with clarity preserves the relationship and your regulation. Use the phrase, *'Let's take a 20-minute pause so we don't cause more harm. I want to come back to this.'*

De-escalation isn't surrender—it's strategy. The most grounded person in the room becomes the emotional anchor.

COACH'S INSIGHT

In high-stakes situations, the best tool isn't what you say—it's having a well-regulated nervous system. If you're regulated, your words will follow. One executive client practiced three breaths before any difficult email or meeting. Over time, her team reported a noticeable shift in tone and morale.

An ER nurse I coached used the phrase *'I'm overloaded—I need 10 minutes to think'* as a self-regulation line in high-pressure team disputes. It bought her space, and surprisingly, earned respect.

RESEARCH SPOTLIGHT

Studies by Gross (2002) on emotional regulation confirm that strategies like 'cognitive reappraisal' (taking time to reflect and reframe an interaction) and 'situational modification' (altering the interaction to create difference, processing time and reflection) reduce both physical stress responses and interpersonal aggression.

CASE STUDY

A couple on the brink of divorce implemented the 90-second pause rule. Arguments that used to last hours now defused in under 5 minutes. Calm and regulated nervous systems lead to more productive conflict resolution.

Exercise 70: Your De-Escalation Plan (Section 16.2)

Create your own de-escalation plan:

1. What are your early signs of escalation (physical or emotional)?

　_____

　_____

2. Which of the de-escalation tools will you try first?

　_____

　_____

3. Who in your life can support you during or after a conflict?

　_____

　_____

Journal Prompt:

- Reflect on a recent conflict. Which tool might have helped reduce intensity?
- What interrupted your ability to regulate in that moment?

16.3 TEMPLATES FOR REPAIR, BOUNDARIES, AND CLARIFYING NEEDS

Rupture Repair Template

- *'I realize that what I said/did hurt you. I want to understand more and take ownership where I need to. Can we talk about it?'*
- *'Looking back, I see how that landed. I didn't mean to cause harm, but I accept that I did.'*

Boundary-Setting Template:

- *'When [identify a behavior] happens, I feel [name an emotion]. What I need moving forward is [set a boundary].'*
- *'I want this relationship to work, and part of that means protecting my peace and clarity.'*
- *'I care about this relationship, and I want to stay connected. That's why I need this boundary respected.'*

Needs Clarification Template:

- 'What I really needed in that moment was [core need: support, respect, understanding].'

- 'Can we talk about how we can meet each other's needs better moving forward?'

These templates allow people to share vulnerable truths without fumbling. They give structure to emotional complexity. Rehearse them until the language becomes natural. They don't make the conversation easy—they make it possible.

COACH'S INSIGHT

One high-achieving client used the boundary template in a team email to set limits around weekend expectations. It immediately shifted the team dynamic and opened space for others to voice their needs.

RESEARCH SPOTLIGHT

Brené Brown's work on boundaries (Dare to Lead, 2018) emphasizes that *clear is kind—unclear is unkind.* Clarity in stating needs and boundaries prevents resentment and miscommunication.

CASE STUDY

After years of avoiding conflict with her sister, a client used the 'rupture-repair' script to open a conversation. That call reopened a relationship they both wanted but didn't know how to repair.

A founder-client used the boundary template after repeated interruptions by others in leadership meetings: *'When I'm cut off mid-sentence, I feel disregarded. What I need moving forward is to finish my point before responses begin.'* The interruptions stopped—and so did his silent resentment.

Exercise 71: Your Go-To De-Escalation Templates (Section 16.3)

Fill in the blank using the following templates:

Boundary:

'When _____ [specific behavior] happens, I feel _____ [emotion]. What I need moving forward is _____ _____ [boundary].'

Repair:

'I realize _____ [describe what happened]. I want to take ownership and hear your experience. Can we talk?'

Needs:

'What I needed in that moment was _____ __ [specific need].'

Journal Prompt:

- Which template do you avoid using, and why?

- How would your most important relationship shift if you used one of these regularly?

SECTION 17:
YOUR CONFLICT MASTERY PLAN

'And once the storm is over, you won't remember how you made it through… But one thing is certain: when you come out of the storm, you won't be the same person who walked in. That's what the storm is all about.'
~ Haruki Murakami

'Decide what kind of life you really want and then say no to everything that isn't that.'
~ Melanie Mackie

"You don't become confident by shouting affirmations in the mirror, but by showing the world irrefutable proof that you are who you say you are".
~ Alex Hormozi

17.1 REFLECTING ON YOUR JOURNEY

Completing this workbook is more than an intellectual achievement—it's a personal transformation. You've examined your triggers, rewritten conflict scripts, and taken bold steps toward relational repair and resilience. You've unlearned outdated responses, faced difficult truths, and integrated healthier patterns of communication and self-regulation.

Now, we consolidate that learning. Reflection isn't indulgence—it's integration. Without reflection, we repeat. With it, we evolve.

This moment is an invitation to pause and absorb your growth.

- What have you noticed about yourself?

_____

- Where do you now pause instead of react?

_____

- What core needs are you no longer afraid to name?

  _____

- Which relationships feel less emotionally chaotic?

  _____

- What inner beliefs about conflict have shifted?

  _____

RESEARCH SPOTLIGHT

Studies in behavior change (Prochaska & DiClemente, 1983) show that the 'maintenance' stage is sustained not by discipline alone, but by identity integration. You are becoming the kind of person who moves through conflict differently. You're not only **DOING** things differently, you **ARE** a different person than you used to be!

17.2 YOUR PERSONAL COMMITMENT STATEMENT

Conflict mastery is a daily decision. It requires intentionality. Your personal commitment statement is a declaration to your future self—a compass to guide you when the old pull toward reactivity arises.

Your personal commitment statement anchors your growth in values and intention. Think of it as your north star for staying grounded when things get messy.

Examples:

> *'I commit to meeting conflict with curiosity, not control. I will validate before I argue, pause before I attack, and lead with clarity instead of fear.'*

> *'I commit to staying present in hard moments, even when I want to run.'*

> *'I will value repair over righteousness, connection over control.'*

RESEARCH SPOTLIGHT

According to ACT (Acceptance and Commitment Therapy) research, value-based commitments enhance emotional regulation by aligning actions with identity (Hayes et al., 2006).

Exercise 72: Your Personal Commitment Statement (Section 17.2)

Write your own statement using language that inspires you. Revisit it when old patterns resurface. Write it. Rehearse it. Post it where you'll see it. Your commitment becomes your anchor.

Reflect on what you've learned about yourself and your relationships.

- What values matter most to you during conflict?
- How do you want to show up when things get hard?

Write your personal commitment statement here:

I commit to:

_____

_____

_____

_____

Journal Prompt:

- What emotion rises when you read your statement aloud?
- How will you remind yourself of this commitment weekly?

17.3 WHY MEASURING GOALS MATTERS FOR REAL CHANGE

Without measurement, growth becomes anecdotal. You may *feel* like you're improving—or not—but subjective impressions often miss the truth. Measuring goals gives structure to your transformation. It helps you track what's working, what isn't, and where to redirect your energy.

Measurement does **three powerful things** in the context of conflict mastery:

1. **Creates Accountability**

    If you say you want to set better boundaries but never check in on how that's going, the intention loses power. Measurable goals create a feedback loop: you set, act, reflect, and recalibrate.

2. **Builds Motivation Through Visible Progress**

   Even small wins matter. When you check a box that says, *'I responded instead of reacted,'* you send a message to your nervous system: *'I'm capable.'* Motivation thrives on evidence—not just emotion.

3. **Shifts Identity From 'Trying' to 'Becoming'**

   Research shows that when people track progress toward goals, they begin to see themselves differently—not as someone who's just *trying* to change, but as someone who *is* changing. That identity shift locks in long-term transformation.

RESEARCH SPOTLIGHT

Goal monitoring increases the likelihood of behavioral follow-through by up to 40% (Harkin et al., 2016, *Psychological Bulletin*). The more frequently individuals reflect on and measure their progress, the more likely they are to sustain meaningful change over time.

COACH'S INSIGHT

One client tracked his weekly use of the V.E.N.T. Method™ during team conflicts. After six weeks, he shared: *'I didn't realize how far I'd come until I saw it on paper.'* Measurement helped him stop minimizing his growth.

Exercise 73: Self-Assessment (Section 17.3)

After completing your self-assessment checklist (Section 17.5, Exercise 76), ask:

- What surprised me about my growth?

  _____
  _____
  _____
  _____

- Where am I still holding back, and why?

  _____
  _____

Use these insights to shape your next 30-day goal.

17.4 GOAL-SETTING PROMPTS

Behavior change happens through consistent micro-actions, not grand declarations. Behavioral momentum comes from specific, repeated actions. Set 30-day goals that feel both ambitious and realistic.

These prompts help you map your continued growth:

- One conflict skill I will practice weekly is:

___

- One relationship I want to repair or deepen is:

___

- One boundary I will reinforce consistently is:

___

- One phrase I'll use to de-escalate tension is:

___

- One support system I'll lean on more consistently is:

___

- One thing I'll let go of (e.g., people-pleasing, control, avoidance):

  _____

  _____

- One limiting belief I will release is:

  _____

  _____

RESEARCH SPOTLIGHT

Studies in goal attainment (Locke & Latham, 2002) confirm that specific, measurable, and emotionally resonant goals are significantly more likely to be achieved than vague resolutions.

Exercise 74: Your 30-Day Growth Goal (Section 17.4)

Choose one conflict skill to practice intentionally over the next 30 days.

- Example: Using the V.E.N.T. method during weekly check-ins with your partner
- Example: Pausing for 10 seconds before responding to difficult emails

  My 30-Day Growth Goal:

  I will practice _____ (conflict skill) every _____ (frequency) with _____ (the identified person in your life).

Journal Prompt:

- What support do you need to follow through?
- What obstacle might come up—and how will you respond?

17.5 SELF-ASSESSMENT CHECKLIST

To promote and sustain growth, it is critical to periodically measure integration, assess your growth and identify new growth areas. Growth isn't linear—but it is trackable.

RESEARCH SPOTLIGHT

Self-monitoring is one of the top predictors of sustained behavior change (Bandura, 1991). When we track progress with compassion, we increase motivation and emotional flexibility.

Exercise 75: Self-Assessment Checklist Review (Section 17.5)

Use this checklist not to judge, but to gain insight and redirect with compassion.

Rate each item as:

✓ = Consistently true   ~ = Sometimes true   ✗ = Needs work

- ☐ I respond instead of reacting in conflict situations
- ☐ I name my core emotional needs clearly and calmly
- ☐ I regularly use validation and curiosity (before persuasion) during disagreements
- ☐ I take breaks to de-escalate instead of powering through
- ☐ I set boundaries with clarity, not apology
- ☐ I have at least one repaired relationship I'm proud of
- ☐ I maintain daily or weekly habits that support emotional regulation
- ☐ I track emotional patterns and revisit my commitment regularly

Journal Prompt:

- What item on the checklist are you most proud of?
- What's your next edge of growth?

A coaching client who had once avoided conflict entirely shared this final reflection: *'For the first time in my life, I feel like I can have hard conversations without losing myself or the relationship.'*

That's the heart of this work—not perfect relationships, but empowered ones. Not avoiding conflict but being transformed by how we move through it.

SECTION 18:
FINAL REFLECTIONS & NEXT STEPS

You've arrived here with a new set of tools — not just for handling conflict, but for transforming it into something more: a source of connection, self-respect, and clarity. You've done the work. You've wrestled with old patterns, stared down discomfort, and chosen to show up differently. This isn't just a workbook anymore — it's a mirror of the person you've become.

RECAP OF THE V.E.N.T. METHOD™

You now hold in your hands a framework that works in boardrooms, breakrooms, living rooms, and anywhere human tension exists.

- **V** = Validate the Emotion: You learned that acknowledgment opens doors faster than argument.

- **E** = Engage Curiously: You replaced assumptions with questions to reveal truth.

- **N** = Navigate Needs: You discovered that unmet needs are the silent engine of most conflicts.

- **T** = Transform: You shifted from reacting to repairing, building resilience with every interaction.

The V.E.N.T. Method™ isn't just a set of steps — it's a way of moving through life. It's the difference between being pulled into chaos and becoming the calm in the center of it.

WHO YOU'VE BECOME THROUGH THIS WORK

If you've truly engaged with these pages, you are no longer the same person who began this journey.

You are clear.

You are steady.

You are more intentional in your words, more grounded in your boundaries, and more strategic in your emotional responses.

Conflict doesn't scare you anymore — it challenges you. It calls you to rise into your best self. And each time you do, you send a signal to everyone around you: this is how we do conflict differently.

YOUR GROWTH ISN'T JUST YOURS: SPREADING THE CHANGE

I invite you to reflect on something I heard from a pastor while writing this workbook. The pear tree doesn't live on pears; the apple tree doesn't live on apples. They live on water. The fruit isn't for the tree; the fruit is for the people who pass by. This is why you can be struggling in your own life, while simultaneously giving someone else advice that changes theirs. Your gifts are not for you; they are for the people who engage with and orbit your life.

The greatest flex is having a well-regulated nervous system. Living an emotionally well-regulated life is a fantastic gift to give to others, just like the fruit tree – it's a gift for others as much, or more, than for you.

Your transformation doesn't stop with you. Every relationship you touch — your partner, your children, your friends, your colleagues — now benefits from the work you've done here.

You've shifted the dynamic. You've modeled what it means to lead without domination, to stand firm without aggression, to listen without surrendering yourself.

The ripple effect is real. The way you handle one conversation can change the tone of an entire household, a whole team, even a whole culture. You are, in every sense, a catalyst for better human interaction.

INVITATION TO WORK TOGETHER: COACHING SUPPORT

This workbook has given you a foundation — but transformation accelerates when you have a guide walking beside you. If you're ready to deepen your conflict mastery, dissolve long-standing patterns, and build relationships that feel stronger and more aligned than ever, I invite you to work with me directly.

Inside my coaching programs, we take these tools and apply them in your real-world scenarios — with tailored strategies, live role-play, and ongoing accountability so that change doesn't just happen in theory, but in the moments that matter most.

Visit: www.theunstressedexec.com

Follow & connect with me:

Instagram → @the.unstressed.exec   TikTok → @the.unstressed.exec

YouTube → @The_Unstressed_Exec   Facebook → The Unstressed Exec

I've spent my career as both an executive coach and a clinical and forensic psychologist, working with leaders, high-achieving professionals, and individuals navigating some of life's most difficult transitions. I know firsthand that conflict — whether in the boardroom or at the dinner table — is rarely just about the moment you're in. It's about the patterns you've carried, the fears you've hidden, and the identity you're ready to step into.

My mission is to help you navigate those moments with strength, clarity, and confidence — so you can create a life, career, and relationships that feel aligned and unshakable.

Your next chapter begins now. Let's write it together.

George J. V. Vergolias, PsyD
CEO | Executive & Life Coach

ABOUT THE AUTHOR

Dr. George Vergolias is an internationally recognized authority in executive coaching, corporate consulting, and clinical/forensic psychology. With over two decades of experience at the intersection of leadership performance, workplace resilience, and human behavior, he has earned a reputation as a trusted advisor to executives, high achievers, organizations, and communities navigating their most high-stakes moments.

As the Chief Clinical Officer of an international company specializing in workplace resilience, Dr. Vergolias helps Fortune 500 companies and global organizations build psychologically safe, resilient workplaces that thrive in the face of disruption. He is also the founder and principal of The Unstressed Exec, a coaching and consulting firm dedicated to helping leaders and high-achievers break free from burnout, master conflict, and lead with clarity and confidence.

A Certified Threat Manager and one of fewer than 100 professionals worldwide to hold both a doctorate in forensic psychology and this elite certification, Dr. Vergolias has assessed/managed more than 1,000 cases of violence risk, self-harm, and crisis events—including active shooter threats, predatory violence, stalking, and workplace safety crises. He also founded TelePsych Supports, a pioneering telehealth company providing crisis consultation and resilience planning to hospitals and emergency departments.

Dr. Vergolias earned his doctorate in Clinical Psychology from The Chicago School of Professional Psychology, completed his clinical internship at Duke University Medical Center/Durham VA Medical Center, and received post-doctoral training in forensic psychology affiliated with the University of Notre Dame. He is an active voice on national advisory boards shaping best practices in risk mitigation, conflict management, and resilience building.

Whether coaching a high achiever or CEO through a career-defining transition, guiding an organization through crisis, or teaching professionals how to master conflict in their personal lives, Dr. Vergolias brings a rare blend of clinical insight, strategic clarity, and no-BS coaching that transforms people and organizations from the inside out.

You can connect with him at george@theunstressedexec.com.

ADDENDUM 1: TOOLS, TEMPLATES & RESOURCES

You've done the deep work of understanding conflict, rewiring how you respond, and learning how to turn difficult moments into turning points. But lasting change isn't just about insight — it's about *implementation*. And implementation gets a whole lot easier when you have the right tools at your fingertips.

This section isn't theory. It's not another lecture. It's your *go bag* — the set of practical, ready-to-use resources that you can grab in the heat of the moment or use in your daily routine to keep your skills sharp and your mindset clear.

Think of it like a gym membership for your conflict management muscles:

- You wouldn't expect to get fit by working out once, and you can't expect your conflict skills to stay sharp without practice.
- These tools give you the reps. They make it simple to stay intentional and avoid slipping back into old patterns.

This section is more than a reference guide — it's your insurance policy against backsliding. When emotions run high, when you're tired, when old habits start to creep in… this is where you turn. Every tool here is designed to make conflict management *automatic* — so that the person you've worked so hard to become is the person who shows up every time.

CONFLICT CONVERSATION STARTERS

Sometimes the hardest part isn't knowing what to say *next* — it's knowing how to start.

These openers help you break the ice, set the tone, and guide even high-stakes conversations toward resolution rather than escalation. They're your shortcut to bypassing awkwardness and getting to the heart of the matter without setting off defensiveness.

Use these to open a difficult conversation with curiosity and calm:

- ☐ *'I want to understand your perspective — can we talk about what happened?'*
- ☐ *'Something's been on my mind, and I'd like to hear your thoughts.'*
- ☐ *'Can we explore what went wrong so we can prevent it in the future?'*
- ☐ *'I respect your opinion and want to find a way forward together.'*
- ☐ *'I may have misunderstood — can you share more about how you see it?'*

30-DAY CONFLICT TRIGGER TRACKER

Growth is easier to track when you can see it on paper. This simple, structured trigger tracker journal helps you reflect on real-life interactions, spot patterns in your triggers, and measure how you're improving. Thirty days from now, you'll be able to look back and see a clear story of your progress — not just in what you *did*, but in who you've *become*.

Date	Situation/Trigger	My Response	The Outcome	Lesson Learned

BOUNDARY SETTING SCRIPTS

Boundaries don't have to be confrontational. Done right, they are simply clarity in action.

These scripts help you say 'yes' to what matters most and 'no' without apology or guilt. Whether you're setting a new limit with a partner, a boss, or a family member, you'll have language that is firm, respectful, and entirely your own.

Adapt these scripts to your own voice. They're designed to be firm, respectful, and clear:

- ☐ 'I'm not able to take that on right now. I can help next week.'
- ☐ 'I value our relationship, and I need to set a limit on discussing this topic.'
- ☐ 'I can't commit to that deadline, but here's what I can do instead.'
- ☐ 'It's important for me to have some time to myself this weekend.'
- ☐ 'I understand your request, but I need to say no to protect my other commitments.'

THE CONFLICT CHECKLIST

This quick-reference list lets you scan for the essentials before entering any high-stakes conversation. It's the small, intentional preparation steps like these that keep a conversation from derailing.

Review this checklist before entering a high-stakes conversation:

- ☐ Am I clear on my desired outcome?
- ☐ Do I know my non-negotiables?
- ☐ Have I prepared at least three open-ended questions?
- ☐ Am I prepared to listen without interrupting?
- ☐ Have I considered the other person's possible needs and perspective?
- ☐ Have I planned how to remain calm if emotions rise?

Guided Role-Play Scenarios

These guided scenarios are designed to help you practice applying the principles of this chapter in realistic, emotionally charged situations. Each scenario includes background context, character perspectives, suggested language, and debrief prompts to deepen learning.

Scenario 1: Setting a Boundary with a Colleague

Background

You have a colleague who frequently drops last-minute work on your desk, expecting you to handle it immediately.

Your Goal

Set a clear boundary without damaging the relationship.

Practice Script

Colleague: *'Hey, can you take care of this report for me? I need it by tomorrow.'*

You: *'I understand it's important. I can take it on if it's due next week, but I'm at capacity today and tomorrow.'*

Colleague: *'But it's urgent.'*

You: *'I wish I could help right now, but I can't commit to urgent turnarounds without notice. Let's plan for next time so I can prioritize it.'*

Debrief Prompts

- How did it feel to state your limit clearly?
- What body language or tone helped communicate your respect and firmness?

Scenario 2: Forgiveness Without Closure in a Friendship

Background

A close friend ghosted you after a disagreement. Months have passed with no explanation.

Your Goal

Release resentment and move forward without needing an apology.

Practice Script

Write (but don't send) a message: *'I was hurt when our communication ended so abruptly. I'm choosing to release that hurt and wish you well.'*

Debrief Prompts

- What emotions came up as you wrote your message?

- How does choosing forgiveness without closure shift your energy or perspective?

Scenario 3: Creating a Conflict Culture in a Team Meeting

Background

Your team tends to avoid speaking up when they disagree with leadership decisions.

Your Goal

Model openness to disagreement and invite constructive feedback.

Practice Script

Leader: *'Before we finalize, I want to hear any concerns or different perspectives. Your input helps us get the best outcome.'*

Team: *'I'm worried this approach could delay our launch.'*

Leader: *'Thank you for raising that. Let's explore what adjustments could keep us on track while addressing that risk.'*

Debrief Prompts

- How did the leader's language create psychological safety?
- What phrases could you use to encourage more open dialogue?

Scenario 4: Using Conflict as Intimacy in a Romantic Relationship

Background

Your partner feels you've been distracted lately and not present in conversations.

Your Goal

Acknowledge their feelings and repair trust.

Practice Script

Partner: *'You're always on your phone when we talk.'*

You: *'I can see why you'd feel dismissed when I'm not giving you full attention.'*

Partner: *'It makes me feel like I don't matter.'*

You: *'You do matter. I want to rebuild our connection. Can we set phone-free time during dinner?'*

Debrief Prompts

- Which part of your response validated your partner's feelings?
- What repair step did you offer, and how might it help?

Scenario 5: Building Your Personal Conflict Playbook in Real Time

Background

In a heated discussion, you feel yourself getting defensive.

Your Goal

Use one of your pre-rehearsed calming techniques and an open-ended question to de-escalate.

Practice Script

Pause, take two deep breaths.

You: *'I want to understand you better. What's the most important part of this for you?'*

Debrief Prompts

- How did pausing before responding affect the tone of the conversation?
- Which playbook tool felt most natural, and which needs more practice?

READING LIST AND RECOMMENDED RESOURCES

Mastery doesn't stop here. I've curated a list of books and podcasts that align with what you've learned — so you can keep growing long after you close this workbook. In these sources you'll find the voices, perspectives, and strategies that complement your new skill set and keep you inspired. These lists are not exhaustive, and there are plenty of others out there that can help guide you further on your journey, but these are the ones I find particularly helpful from a perspective of differing voices.

Top Book Recommendations	Top Podcast Recommendations
Nonviolent Communication by Marshall B. Rosenberg	*The Unstressed Exec podcast* Dr. George Vergolias
Crucial Conversations by Patterson, Grenny, McMillan, & Switzler	*Diary of a CEO (DOAC) podcast* Steven Bartlett
Dare to Lead by Brené Brown	*Modern Wisdom podcast* Chris Williamson
The Anatomy of Peace by The Arbinger Institute	*Huberman Lab podcast* Dr. Andrew Huberman
Radical Candor by Kim Scot	**The Drive podcast** Dr. Peter Attia
	The Mel Robbins podcast Mel Robbins

ADDENDUM 2: CITATIONS AND SUMMARY NOTES

Adams, R. G., & Blieszner, R. (1995). Aging well with friends and family. *American Behavioral Scientist, 39*(2), 209–224.

Summary: *The loss of close friendships can lead to loneliness, rumination, and disruptions in self-identity, yet such losses often go unacknowledged and unsupported socially.*

Amato, P. R., & Afifi, T. D. (2006). Feeling caught between parents: Adult children's relations with parents and subjective well-being. *Journal of Marriage and Family, 68*(1), 222–235.

Summary: *This study links high-conflict divorce to chronic anxiety, loyalty conflicts, and impaired emotional regulation in children, effects that can persist well into adulthood.*

American Psychiatric Association. (2013). *Diagnostic and statistical manual of mental disorders* (5th ed.). Arlington, VA: American Psychiatric Publishing.

Summary: *The DSM-5 notes that traits associated with borderline, narcissistic, and paranoid personality disorders frequently appear in high-conflict behaviors. However, it is the recurring interactional patterns, not the diagnostic label, that primarily sustain the conflict dynamic.*

American Psychological Association. (2019). *Managing high-conflict divorce: The role of emotional regulation and attachment repair*. Washington, DC: Author.

Summary: *The APA reports that prolonged high-conflict divorces are more often driven by unresolved emotional injuries and poor emotional regulation than by the legal disputes themselves. These dynamics are frequently rooted in attachment injuries rather than the surface-level issues in contention.*

Association of Family and Conciliation Courts. (2020). *Parent communication patterns and litigation risk in separation and divorce cases*. Madison, WI: AFCC.

Summary: *AFCC research shows that communication style during separation is the strongest predictor of whether parents will enter high-conflict litigation within a year. Consistent, emotionally neutral, and well-documented communication is linked to a significantly reduced likelihood of court escalation.*

Bandura, A. (1991). Social cognitive theory of self-regulation. *Organizational Behavior and Human Decision Processes, 50*(2), 248–287.

Summary: *Bandura's work identifies self-monitoring as one of the strongest predictors of sustained behavior change. Compassionate tracking of progress increases motivation, adaptability, and emotional flexibility over time.*

Baumeister, R. F., Heatherton, T. F., & Tice, D. M. (1994). *Losing control: How and why people fail at self-regulation.* San Diego, CA: Academic Press.

Summary: *Baumeister and colleagues found that unresolved internal conflicts drain mental and emotional energy, leading to burnout and diminished relational resilience. The capacity to reconcile competing aspects of the self is a core component of emotional intelligence.*

Beck, A. T. (1979). *Cognitive therapy and the emotional disorders.* New York, NY: Penguin Books.

Summary: *Beck's foundational work in cognitive behavioral therapy (CBT) demonstrates that cognitive reframing—identifying and replacing unhelpful thought patterns—reduces emotional reactivity and fosters constructive communication, particularly in high-conflict couples.*

Buehler, A. M., Leavitt, C. E., & Allsop, D. B. (2007). Adolescents' cognitive and emotional responses to marital hostility. *Child Development, 78*(3), 775–789.

Summary: *This study found that exposure to marital hostility—reflective of poor emotional boundaries within the family context—was linked to adolescents showing heightened emotional reactivity and diminished emotional regulation. These patterns are associated with poorer relationship functioning and emotional well-being.*

Brown, B. (2012). *Daring greatly: How the courage to be vulnerable transforms the way we live, love, parent, and lead.* New York, NY: Gotham Books.

Summary: *Brown's research distinguishes between guilt (focused on behavior) and shame (focused on self-worth). Healthy guilt motivates repair and fosters empathy, while shame isolates and erodes connection.*

Brown, B. (2018). *Dare to lead: Brave work. Tough conversations. Whole hearts.* New York, NY: Random House.

> *Summary: Brown emphasizes that 'clear is kind, unclear is unkind,' noting that openly stating needs and boundaries fosters trust, reduces resentment, and prevents the miscommunication that can erode relationships.*

Chamberlain, C., & Varvin, S. (2020). Window of tolerance: A framework for working with the arousal system in trauma therapy. *Frontiers in Psychology, 11,* 601518.

> *Summary: Siegel's Window of Tolerance model describes optimal arousal for processing information and engaging effectively in relationships. Chamberlain & Varvin confirmed its clinical relevance across populations, distinguishing between states of resilience and dysregulation.*

Davidson, R. J., & McEwen, B. S. (2012). Social influences on neuroplasticity: Stress and interventions to promote well-being. *Nature Neuroscience, 15*(5), 689–695.

> *Summary: Davidson's work demonstrates that mindfulness training strengthens prefrontal cortex activation and reduces amygdala reactivity. Over time, this leads to improved emotional regulation and reduced stress reactivity.*

Davis, D. E., Ho, M. Y., Griffin, B. J., Bell, C., Hook, J. N., Van Tongeren, D. R., ... & Worthington, E. L., Jr. (2015). Forgiving the self and physical and mental health correlates: A meta-analytic review. *Journal of Counseling Psychology, 62*(2), 329–335.

> *Summary: This meta-analysis found that self-forgiveness is linked to reduced depressive symptoms, greater relationship satisfaction, and higher likelihood of positive behavioral change, underscoring its role in both mental health and relational quality.*

DeDreu, C. K., & Weingart, L. R. (2003). Task versus relationship conflict, team performance, and team member satisfaction: A meta-analysis. *Journal of Applied Psychology, 88*(4), 741–749.

> *Summary: De Dreu & Weingart's meta-analysis found that constructive conflict—debating ideas while preserving respect—enhances innovation and problem-solving.*

Donovan, L. A., & Furlong, M. J. (2022). A meta-analytic review of forgiveness in interpersonal relationships: Predictors, processes, and outcomes. *Clinical Psychology Review, 97,* 102188.

> *Summary: This meta-review concluded that perceived sincerity in repair attempts is the strongest predictor of forgiveness and relational reconnection, outweighing the specific content or method of the repair itself.*

Driskell, J. E., Copper, C., & Moran, A. (1994). Does mental practice enhance performance? *Journal of Applied Psychology, 79*(4), 481–492.

> ***Summary:*** *This meta-analysis found that mental rehearsal—pre-rehearsing coping scripts—activates similar neural pathways as actual performance, improving execution under stress. Such preparation increased constructive engagement in high-pressure situations by up to 50%.*

Duhigg, C. (2016, February 25; 2017). *What Google learned from its quest to build the perfect team.* Harvard Business Review

> ***Summary:*** *Based on Google's 'Project Aristotle,' this article reports that psychological safety is the most critical factor for high-performing teams. Teams that felt safe to openly address conflict and take risks showed higher performance, greater innovation, and lower turnover than teams lacking this environment.*

Eddy, B. (2011). *High conflict people in legal disputes* (2nd ed.). Scottsdale, AZ: High Conflict Institute Press.

> ***Summary:*** *Eddy identifies four core markers of high-conflict personalities (HCPs): all-or-nothing thinking, unmanaged emotions, extreme behaviors, and a persistent focus on blaming others. Early recognition of these traits enables professionals to set preventative boundaries and manage interactions more effectively.*

Eddy, B., & Ungar, A. (2019). *BIFF for co-parent communication: Your guide to difficult texts, emails, and social media posts.* Scottsdale, AZ: High Conflict Institute Press.

> ***Summary:*** *Eddy and Ungar's research support the use of the BIFF model—Brief, Informative, Friendly, Firm—as a structured communication method to reduce emotional escalation in interactions with HCPs. Training in BIFF techniques significantly improves resolution timelines and reduces conflict intensity.*

Edmondson, A. C. (2018; 2019). *The fearless organization: Creating psychological safety in the workplace for learning, innovation, and growth.* Harvard Business Review Press.

> ***Summary:*** *Workplace studies summarized by Edmondson indicate that teams practicing regular post-conflict repair see a 35% increase in psychological safety and higher retention rates. Repair processes strengthen not only interpersonal trust but also overall team performance.*

Eisenberger, N. I., Jarcho, J. M., Lieberman, M. D., & Naliboff, B. D. (2006). An experimental study of shared sensitivity to physical pain and social rejection. *Emotion, 6*(5), 726–738.

Summary: Eisenberger's research demonstrates that perceived social rejection activates many of the same neural pathways as physical pain. This overlap explains why relational threats can feel physically painful and prompt defensive or avoidant behaviors.

Enright, R. D., Freedman, S., & Rique, J. (1998). The psychology of interpersonal forgiveness. In R. D. Enright & J. North (Eds.), *Exploring forgiveness* (pp. 46–62). Madison, WI: University of Wisconsin Press.

Summary: Enright's work demonstrates that structured self-forgiveness interventions can significantly reduce anxiety, anger, and depression—emotions that often escalate interpersonal conflict and block relational repair.

Fehr, B. (2000). The life cycle of friendship. In C. Hendrick & S. S. Hendrick (Eds.), *Close relationships: A sourcebook* (pp. 71–82). Thousand Oaks, CA: Sage.

Summary: Fehr's research shows that unresolved friendship losses can cause levels of distress comparable to romantic breakups, underscoring the need for greater societal recognition of these experiences.

Goleman, D. (1995; 2006). *Emotional intelligence: Why it can matter more than IQ*. New York, NY: Bantam Books.

Summary: Goleman coined the term 'amygdala hijack' to describe intense emotional responses triggered before the brain's rational centers engage, often leading to disproportionate reactions. The term has become a foundational concept in emotional intelligence and conflict management. Goleman explains that during an 'amygdala hijack,' heightened emotional arousal bypasses rational processing, leading individuals—especially HCPs—to misinterpret logical input as threatening or dismissive. Emotional regulation is a prerequisite for constructive dialogue and sound decision-making.

Gordon, A. M., Impett, E. A., Kogan, A., Oveis, C., & Keltner, D. (2021). Small investments: Weekly relationship check-ins enhance relationship quality and satisfaction. *Journal of Social and Personal Relationships, 38*(8), 2276–2295.

Summary: Couples who engaged in brief, weekly check-in conversations reported a 31% reduction in relational tension, increased emotional attunement, and higher satisfaction scores, demonstrating the outsized impact of small, consistent investments in connection.

Gottman, J. M., & Levenson, R. W. (1999). What predicts change in marital interaction over time? A study of alternative models. *Family Process, 38*(2), 143–158.

Summary: Gottman's research shows that in stable, happy relationships, there are at least five positive interactions for every negative one during conflict discussions. Maintaining this ratio protects emotional connection and prevents long-term relational instability.

Gottman, J. M., & Silver, N. (1999). *The seven principles for making marriage work*. Three Rivers Press.

Summary: Gottman's research found that approximately 69% of recurring relationship issues are 'perpetual problems' rooted in personality or value differences. The distinguishing factor in relationship health is not solving every problem but maintaining emotional safety and respect during conflict.

Gross, J. J. (2002). Emotion regulation: Affective, cognitive, and social consequences. *Psychophysiology, 39*(3), 281–291.

Summary: Gross's research on emotional regulation demonstrates that strategies such as cognitive reappraisal—reflecting and reframing interactions—and situational modification—altering the interaction to allow for processing—reduce physiological stress markers and lower interpersonal aggression.

Gross, J. J., & John, O. P. (2003). Individual differences in two emotion regulation processes: Implications for affect, relationships, and well-being. *Journal of Personality and Social Psychology, 85*(2), 348–362.

Summary: This study found that people who habitually suppress emotions experience lower life satisfaction, weaker relationships, and less social support. Chronic suppression also correlates with physiological stress indicators.

Gottman, J. M., & Gottman, J. S. (2015). *10 principles for doing effective couple's therapy*. New York, NY: W. W. Norton & Company.

Summary: The Gottmans' longitudinal research shows that in stable relationships, partners respond positively to repair attempts 86% of the time, compared to less than 30% in distressed couples. The findings emphasize that repair is about the willingness to reconnect, not delivering the perfect words.

Groysberg, B., & Slind, M. (2016, May 4). Why do so many managers avoid giving praise? *Harvard Business Review*.

Summary: Harvard Business Review reported that 70% of managers are uncomfortable communicating with employees, particularly when delivering tough feedback. The article *emphasizes that active listening and clear, respectful dialogue improve trust, engagement, and retention.*

Harkin, B., Webb, T. L., Chang, B. P. I., Prestwich, A., Conner, M., Kellar, I., Benn, Y., & Sheeran, P. (2016). Does monitoring goal progress promote goal attainment? A meta-analysis of the experimental evidence. *Psychological Bulletin, 142*(2), 198–229.

Summary: This meta-analysis found that monitoring progress toward goals increases the likelihood of attainment by up to 40%. Frequent reflection and measurement significantly enhance persistence and follow-through.

Hayes, S. C., Luoma, J. B., Bond, F. W., Masuda, A., & Lillis, J. (2006). Acceptance and commitment therapy: Model, processes, and outcomes. *Behavior Research and Therapy, 44*(1), 1–25.

Summary: ACT research demonstrates that committing to values-based actions enhances emotional regulation and resilience. By aligning behavior with deeply held values, individuals foster identity congruence and sustained change.

Higgins, E. T. (1987). Self-discrepancy: A theory relating self and affect. *Psychological Review, 94*(3), 319–340.

Summary: Higgins' self-discrepancy theory explains that emotional distress occurs when there's a gap between the 'actual self' and the 'ideal' or 'ought' self. Bridging that gap with self-compassion, rather than self-punishment, is key to emotional well-being.

Hochschild, A. R. (1983). *The managed heart: Commercialization of human feeling.* Berkeley, CA: University of California Press.

Summary: Hochschild's foundational work revealed that women—particularly in service or caregiving roles—are often expected to manage others' emotions while suppressing their own, a dynamic linked to emotional exhaustion and resentment. Nadal and colleagues extend this to show how intersecting identity factors can compound emotional labor demands.

Johnson, S. M. (2008). *Hold me tight: Seven conversations for a lifetime of love.* New York, NY: Little, Brown Spark.

Summary: Johnson's Emotionally Focused Therapy framework identifies that most relationship conflict—estimated at around 70%—is rooted in unmet attachment needs such as security, emotional accessibility, and feeling valued. Addressing these needs can de-escalate conflict cycles.

Kabat-Zinn, J. (1994). *Wherever you go, there you are: Mindfulness meditation in everyday life.* New York, NY: Hyperion.

> *Summary: Kabat-Zinn's work shows that mindfulness cultivates meta-cognition—the ability to observe thoughts without identifying with them. This reduces emotional reactivity and allows for more intentional, choice-driven responses in conflict.*

Kashdan, T. B., Goodman, F. R., Disabato, D. J., & Kaufman, S. B. (2022). Emotional awareness and regulation: A meta-analytic review of interventions for improving emotional intelligence. *Emotion Review, 14*(3), 155–170.

> *Summary: This meta-analysis found that interventions focused on early recognition of emotional cues significantly reduced the likelihood of emotional escalation. The benefit was tied more to speed of awareness and regulation than to the intensity of the trigger itself.*

Kelly, J. B., & Emery, R. E. (2003). Children's adjustment following divorce: Risk and resilience perspectives. *Family Relations, 52*(4), 352–362.

> *Summary: This review found that the level of parental conflict during and after divorce is a stronger predictor of children's long-term psychological adjustment than the divorce itself, with high-conflict cases posing the greatest risk.*

Kluwer, E. S., Karremans, J. C., Riedijk, L., & Knee, C. R. (2021). Power, conflict, and cooperation in intimate relationships: A meta-analysis. *Journal of Family Psychology, 35*(4), 531–545.

> *Summary: This meta-analysis found that perceived power imbalances in intimate relationships correlate strongly with heightened physiological stress, lower relationship satisfaction, and poorer conflict resolution outcomes. Emotional safety is a key mediator in these dynamics.*

LeDoux, J. E. (1996). *The emotional brain: The mysterious underpinnings of emotional life.* New York, NY: Simon & Schuster.

> *Summary: LeDoux's neuroscience research shows the amygdala can initiate a threat response in as little as 12 milliseconds, while cortical processing for rational thought takes around 300 milliseconds. This explains why emotional reactions can occur before conscious awareness or control.*

Locke, E. A., & Latham, G. P. (2002). Building a practically useful theory of goal setting and task motivation: A 35-year odyssey. *American Psychologist, 57*(9), 705–717.

Summary: Locke and Latham's goal-setting theory confirms that specific, measurable, and emotionally meaningful goals produce higher achievement rates than vague intentions, by focusing attention and increasing commitment.

McEwen, B. S., & Gianaros, P. J. (2010). Central role of the brain in stress and adaptation: Links to socioeconomic status, health, and disease. *Annals of the New York Academy of Sciences, 1186*(1), 190–222.

Summary: McEwen and Gianaros describe 'allostatic load' as the cumulative wear on the body's systems caused by chronic stress. They found that unresolved emotional strain, particularly from conflict, erodes physical and psychological health over time, while supportive relationships and healthy routines act as protective buffers.

Mikulincer, M., & Shaver, P. R. (2007). *Attachment in adulthood: Structure, dynamics, and change.* New York, NY: Guilford Press.

Summary: This work synthesizes decades of attachment research, showing how early caregiver relationships shape adult patterns of intimacy, trust, and conflict. Insecure attachment styles—anxious or avoidant—often lead to conflict behaviors driven by fear of abandonment or discomfort with closeness.

Mikulincer, M., & Shaver, P. R. (2016). *Attachment in adulthood: Structure, dynamics, and change* (2nd ed.). New York, NY: Guilford Press.

Summary: Attachment research shows that securely attached individuals tend to approach conflict with openness and problem-solving, while anxious partners often escalate in fear of abandonment and avoidant partners tend to withdraw or shut down to reduce discomfort.

Nadal, K. L., Mazzula, S. L., Rivera, D. P., & Fujii-Doe, W. (2014). Microaggressions and the public sector workplace: Experiences of racial and ethnic minority psychologists. *The Psychologist-Manager Journal, 17*(3), 182–201.

Summary: Hochschild's foundational work revealed that women—particularly in service or caregiving roles—are often expected to manage others' emotions while suppressing their own, a dynamic linked to emotional exhaustion and resentment. Nadal and colleagues extend this to show how intersecting identity factors can compound emotional labor demands.

Neff, K. D. (2003). Self-compassion: An alternative conceptualization of a healthy attitude toward oneself. *Self and Identity, 2*(2), 85–101.

Summary: *Neff's foundational research shows that harsh self-judgment correlates with increased anxiety, depression, and emotional reactivity—all of which intensify interpersonal conflict. Self-kindness, by contrast, promotes resilience and emotional stability.*

Neff, K. D., & Germer, C. K. (2013). A pilot study and randomized controlled trial of the mindful self-compassion program. *Journal of Clinical Psychology, 69*(1), 28–44.

Summary: *This study found that an eight-week mindful self-compassion program significantly reduced self-criticism and increased emotional resilience across varied populations. Understanding and softening the inner critic expanded participants' capacity for self-support. They also found that people who cultivate self-kindness recover faster from emotional wounds and display greater resilience in relationships.*

Nicolaides, V. C., & Tull, M. T. (2022). The 'fawn' response: Understanding appeasement behavior in the context of trauma. *Psychological Trauma: Theory, Research, Practice, and Policy, 14*(5), 879–888.

Summary: *This study identified fawn responses—appeasing or people-pleasing under threat—as linked to early attachment injury and disproportionately present in high-conflict relationships involving trauma histories. The findings expand trauma theory to include appeasement as a survival strategy.*

Nie, Y., Chua, B. L., Yeung, A. S., Ryan, R. M., & Chan, W. Y. (2017). The importance of autonomy support and the mediating role of work motivation for well-being: Testing self-determination theory in a Chinese work organization. *Frontiers in Psychology, 8*, 1731.

Summary: *This study found that individuals with clear personal boundaries reported lower stress and anxiety, greater self-esteem, higher relationship satisfaction, and improved conflict resolution outcomes. Boundaries function as protective buffers, lowering emotional reactivity and reducing interpersonal friction.*

Porges, S. W. (2011). *The polyvagal theory: Neurophysiological foundations of emotions, attachment, communication, and self-regulation.* New York, NY: W. W. Norton & Company.

Summary: *Porges' Polyvagal Theory explains how the vagus nerve regulates feelings of safety, connection, and defense. A well-regulated nervous system promotes social engagement, while a dysregulated system primes the body for fight, flight, or shutdown even in the absence of real danger. Polyvagal Theory highlights that perceived safety—especially internal safety—is essential for emotional regulation and social connection. Without it, individuals remain in a state of hypervigilance or shutdown.*

Prochaska, J. O., & DiClemente, C. C. (1983). Stages and processes of self-change of smoking: Toward an integrative model of change. *Journal of Consulting and Clinical Psychology, 51*(3), 390–395.

> ***Summary:*** *Prochaska and DiClemente's transtheoretical model shows that the 'maintenance' stage of behavior change is sustained not solely through discipline, but through identity integration—becoming the kind of person who naturally engages in the new behavior.*

Remland, M. S., Jones, T. S., & Brinkman, H. (2020). Nonverbal communication and conflict in workplace interactions. *Journal of Conflict Resolution, 64*(7-8), 1315–1342.

> ***Summary:*** *This study found that over 65% of workplace disputes originated from perceptions of tone, facial expressions, or body language rather than the substantive content of the message. Misinterpretation of nonverbal cues was a primary conflict driver.*

Rotenberg, K. J. (2010). *Interpersonal trust during childhood and adolescence.* Cambridge University Press.

> ***Summary:*** *Rotenberg's work highlights that self-trust is built on congruence between one's thoughts, feelings, and actions. Strengthening this internal alignment enhances decision-making and emotional stability.*

Rozovsky, J. (2015, November 17). *The five keys to a successful Google team.* re: Work.

> ***Summary:*** *Google's multi-year study of team performance found that psychological safety was the single strongest predictor of team success. Teams that openly addressed tension and mistakes outperformed those that avoided conflict.*

Schwartz, R. C. (2001). *Internal family systems therapy.* New York, NY: Guilford Press.

> ***Summary:*** *Schwartz's Internal Family Systems model holds that every inner part, even critical ones, serves a protective purpose. Sustainable change comes from acknowledging and working with these parts instead of suppressing or attacking them.*

Siegel, D. J. (1999). *The developing mind: Toward a neurobiology of interpersonal experience.* New York, NY: Guilford Press.

> ***Summary:*** *Siegel's Window of Tolerance model describes optimal arousal for processing information and engaging effectively in relationships. Chamberlain & Varvin confirmed its clinical relevance across populations, distinguishing between states of resilience and dysregulation.*

Siegel, D. J. (2010). *The mindful therapist: A clinician's guide to mindsight and neural integration.* New York, NY: W. W. Norton & Company.

Summary: Siegel introduces the concept of 'flipping your lid' to illustrate how emotional reactivity occurs when the amygdala overrides the prefrontal cortex. This temporary loss of rational control explains why conflict can feel overwhelming in the moment and highlights the importance of regulation skills.

Srivastava, S., Tamir, M., McGonigal, K. M., John, O. P., & Gross, J. J. (2009). The social costs of emotional suppression: A prospective study of the transition to college. *Journal of Personality and Social Psychology, 96*(4), 883–897.

Summary: This longitudinal study showed that habitual emotional suppression predicted fewer positive social interactions and greater depressive symptoms over time. Suppression undermines relationship quality and psychological well-being.

Stone, D., Patton, B., & Heen, S. (2019). *Difficult conversations: How to discuss what matters most* (3rd ed.). New York, NY: Penguin Books.

Summary: Drawing from Harvard Negotiation Project findings, the authors report that concise, boundary-based statements are perceived as more trustworthy and emotionally intelligent than lengthy justifications, particularly in high-stakes or emotionally charged discussions.

Suler, J. (2004). The online disinhibition effect. *CyberPsychology & Behavior, 7*(3), 321–326.

Summary: Suler's work describes how anonymity and lack of face-to-face interaction online can reduce empathy and increase aggression, making digital conflicts more emotionally intense and harder to resolve constructively.

Tannen, D. (1990). *You just don't understand: Women and men in conversation.* New York, NY: Ballantine Books.

Summary: Tannen's research found that many conflicts in couples stem not from substantive disagreements but from differences in conversational style and interpretation. These differences often reflect mismatched goals — for example, one partner seeking connection while the other aims to problem-solve — creating tension even when values align.

Tronick, E. Z., Als, H., Adamson, L., Wise, S., & Brazelton, T. B. (1978). The infant's response to entrapment between contradictory messages in face-to-face interaction. *Journal of the American Academy of Child Psychiatry, 17*(1), 1–13.

Summary: Tronick's 'Still-Face Experiment' demonstrated that infants rely heavily on responsive, nonverbal co-regulation for emotional stability. When caregivers abruptly stop responding, infants quickly show signs of distress, highlighting the critical role of attunement in emotional development.

Tugade, M. M., & Fredrickson, B. L. (2004). Resilient individuals use positive emotions to bounce back from negative emotional experiences. *Journal of Personality and Social Psychology, 86*(2), 320–333.

> ***Summary:*** *Tugade and Fredrickson found that resilient individuals use positive emotions and reflective coping strategies to recover more quickly from stress. These individuals also show greater emotional regulation and cognitive reappraisal—key skills for reducing conflict and sustaining healthy relationships.*

Wass, S. V., Whitehorn, M., Haresign, I. M., Phillips, E., & Leong, V. (2021). Interpersonal neural entrainment during early social interaction. *Trends in Cognitive Sciences, 25*(5), 347–359.

> ***Summary:*** *This research found that co-regulated interactions between dyads can lead to synchronized heart rate variability, a sign of physiological alignment. Such synchronization supports emotional security and resilience.*

Williamson, H. C., Altman, N., Hsueh, J., & Bradbury, T. N. (2019). Effects of communication training and practice on newlywed couples' communication skills and satisfaction. *Journal of Social and Personal Relationships, 36*(11-12), 3502–3524.

> ***Summary:*** *This study found that couples who engaged in consistent post-conflict repair behaviors reported higher emotional intimacy, greater confidence in handling disagreements, and reduced emotional withdrawal over time.*

Wilson, S. R., & Gallois, C. (1993). Assertion and its social context. *Advances in experimental social psychology, 26*, 1–39.

> ***Summary:*** *This meta-analysis found that assertiveness—expressing one's needs and opinions clearly while respecting others—was positively associated with psychological well-being, interpersonal competence, and leadership effectiveness across various professional settings.*

Worthington, E. L., Jr., & Scherer, M. (2004). Forgiveness is an emotion-focused coping strategy that can reduce health risks and promote health resilience: Theory, review, and hypotheses. *Psychology & Health, 19*(3), 385–405.

> ***Summary:*** *Worthington's REACH Forgiveness model demonstrates that forgiveness, even without reconciliation, lowers stress hormone levels, improves cardiovascular functioning, and enhances psychological well-being. Neuroimaging studies show reduced amygdala activation—the brain's 'threat center'—during forgiveness practices.*

Zaccaro, A., Piarulli, A., Laurino, M., Garbella, E., Menicucci, D., Neri, B., & Gemignani, A. (2018). How breath-control can change your life: A systematic review on psychophysiological correlates of slow breathing. *Frontiers in Human Neuroscience, 12,* 353.

Summary: *This review synthesizes evidence that slow, deep breathing decreases sympathetic nervous system activity and increases vagal tone, improving emotional regulation and resilience. Higher vagal tone is associated with greater adaptability and stress recovery.*

www.ingramcontent.com/pod-product-compliance
Lightning Source LLC
Chambersburg PA
CBHW051351070526
44584CB00025B/3722